TABLE OF CONTENTS

Table of Contents ....

PREFACE...1

CHAPTER 1..3

History and Evolution of the Music Industry.............3

   Summary on the Evolution of the Music Industry... 11

   The Three Key Elements Driving the Evolution of Music and the Music Industry...............................14

   Artists that Have Been Taken Advantage of by Major Record labels 17

   The Negative and Positive Effects of Technology on the Music Industry..31

      Pros..33

      Cons...36

CHAPTER 2...41

What is Indie Music? 41

   When do Indie Artists Need a Manager? 44

   Pros and Cons of Being an Indie Artist.................48

   Tips to Building Your Team as an Indie Musician... 57

   Successful Indie Artists 67

CHAPTER 3 73

Pros and Cons of Signing with Major Record Labels... 73

    Different Types of Recording Contracts 73

    Standard Record Deal 74

    Pros and Cons of 360 Deals 88

    Pros and Cons of Profit Split Record Deals or Net Profit Deals.. 95

    Anti-360 Deals 105

    Artist Deals or Development Deals.................... 106

    Licensing Deal 108

        What Is Licensing?... 108

        What Is Distribution? 109

    Distribution Deal 112

    EP Deals 112

    Major Label Deals 114

    Single Deals.. 114

        Why a single deal? 115

    Ownership of Masters and Publishing 116

    Merchandising.. 118

        Points to Note in Merchandise Deals 119

        Tour Merchandise Advances 121

Chapter 4 123

Recoupable Costs 123

    Recoupable Cost "Major vs. Indie" 123

        Major Label Artist Example............................ 124

- Indie: Indie Artist Example 125
- Tour support "Major vs. Indie" 127
- Indie/Small Record Labels Tour Support 129
- Example of Indie Tour Cost 132
- The Figures 134
- Importance of Social Media when being an Indie Artist 136
  - What does Social Media offer? 137
- Ways you can Use Social Media 138

Chapter 5 142

Revenue 142
- Indie Artists Revenue 143
  - Recording Revenue 143
  - Performance Revenue 151
  - Different Revenue Streams for Artists 153
- Major Record Label Artists Revenue 158

CONCLUSION 166

REFERENCES 168

PREFACE

What does it take to be distinguished as a music artist? How can you build a music career and achieve success in the music industry?

The music business is serious business and it should be approached and treated as such. A successful career in music doesn't happen by wishful thinking, nor does it happen overnight. It takes knowledge, dedication, patience, an open mind and even some failure to clarify your goals and make them happen.

This book will help you understand the challenges and key drivers shaping the music industry, it will guide you on your journey of building your music career, and will ensure that you continue with a good foundation necessary for long term success in the music industry.

CHAPTER 1
HISTORY AND EVOLUTION OF THE MUSIC INDUSTRY

The music industry became a big business in the 20th century. Back in the 1700s and 1800s, music was predominantly financed by the state, wealthy businessmen, the church, or was played in the home by non-professionals.

In the mid-1800s, music began to be produced on a large scale. Songs were considered "hits" if they were part of successful operettas, or if a well-known touring singer or vaudeville performer did the song repeatedly during their tour. Back in the day, someone like Al Jolson was known to include his name as a co-writer on songs so that he would receive royalties in exchange for making the songs famous, even though he did not actually write any lyrics.

Publishers sold thousands of copies of sheet music of "hit songs" to the musically literate so they could be played at home on their pianos. The prospects of producing new songs that could readily capture the public's attention became alluring to publishers and songwriters.

The 20th century saw the expansion of this model of large-scale distribution. There was a high demand for dance bands and published arrangements of popular songs to play for them. Band business, as they were called, became popular between WW1 and WW2. In this period, the technology for recording performances got increasingly better. This resulted in the rapid growth of purchases of record players and albums, thereby opening more avenues for record companies, publishers, writers, and artists to earn more money.

The most significant boom came with the radio. In the 1920s, broadcast networks were started by radio set producers. In the beginning, broadcasts were free but once producers saw the potential in charging for programming, they quickly sold virtually all of them and sought ways to generate new streams of income. Producers soon developed the advertising model that provided support for radio through many generations. Even in the 21st century, it is the model for digital streaming platforms like Spotify.

In addition to paying artists for live performances, this served as an effective tool for newly released songs, musicals, and live appearances. This marked the first time that American audiences could connect to new artists and their songs at the same time.

The 1930s was a period that experienced a plunge in the recording industry. As a result of the Great Depression many Americans preferred radio since it was free. The advent of the new "soundie" technology caused a boom in Hollywood as performers and songwriters began working in "talking pictures." As the world gradually stepped out of the depression in the late '30s, the arrival of swing music prompted young people to patronize records again. The jukebox industry naturally boomed, witnessing increased sales of records. This trend continued until the mid-1940s.

After WW2, soldiers and their lovers began to settle down into domestic life, causing a decline in the dance band business. However, a boom in TV set purchases in the early 1950s provided a new platform for music. The recording industry simultaneously rose again as TV shows and performances by new artists (especially those of the Rock 'n' Roll ilk) served as a catalyst for the industry's success. By eliminating live performances by artists and simply playing their recordings, radio lowered its costs and also captured a large market share. The sheer uniqueness of Rock 'n' Roll (young people were crazy for it) also helped transform the industry.

Initially, composers wrote songs that were performed by artists. Rock 'n' Roll, on the other hand, combined these two into one. Being that these performers were under contract with the record companies, the record companies had more power than the publishers.

As a result of the record companies' ability to shape the industry and control artists with their newfound power, they became a well-oiled corporate juggernaut that reached its peak in the 1980s. The disadvantage of this model was that many middlemen could easily decide what the public listened to. Music now sold on image rather than artistic excellence unbeknownst to vast majority of the public.

Interestingly enough, this model empowered record companies to develop artists. They could easily generate the required support for relatively unknown artists. For example, they could afford to put together a 50-piece orchestra behind an unknown artist and handle whatever losses may come if the artist didn't go on to become a star.

The 1990s saw the decline and subsequent end of the big record companies. First came CDR technology which allowed people to copy CDs. Records were hard to copy to CD, tapes were easier but copies were low in quality (they were difficult to listen to and easily broke). CDs provided a medium to share high-quality music without making payments for it. MP3 soon followed the burned CD, as sharing sites like Napster arrived. These sites allowed people to share recordings quickly and easily - without spending a penny.

In the late 1990s, lawsuits soon worked to shut down these free sharing sites. Before these litigations started, mp3 had become the standard format for listening to music. By 2001, Napster had peaked, having over 25 million users. With this trend and increasing growth in mp3, Apple launched iTunes in 2001, offering a legal platform for the purchase and download of mp3s. This cause the CD to quickly become obsolete. Even today, very few computers have CD drives.

It's no secret that the music industry has been trying to develop various methods to limit the illegal reproduction of music. Bootlegging music costs record labels millions of dollars in revenue annually. The reality is that the music industry has never fully recovered from the illegal file-sharing crisis that dominated the early 2000s. This crisis has forever negatively impacted the music industry.

As a result of the massive loss in album sale revenue thanks to the illegal file-sharing sites such as Napster and LimeWire, the major record labels decided to deduct the lost profits from the artist's other revenue shares in what is called a 360 deal contract (we will consider this in detail later in this book).

People had experienced the joy of free music, and with the advent of the internet and many technological advancements over the years, streaming services began to pop up and compete with platforms that sold mp3s. As a result of these drastic changes in the landscape of the music industry, many record companies began to sell the works of their artists to different digital media retailers.

Throughout the 20th century, large record companies took on the responsibility of taking care of their artists. Some of these companies exist today but no longer have the resources to fulfill their financial responsibilities and complete projects. These record labels took the digital route because it was more cost-efficient and it saved them the headache of worrying about damaged or returned items.

However, the "unmet customer" faced a major problem- they did not have devices to listen to the digital downloads/streams. This happened because in 1999, when digital music content first came out, the only devices capable of playing digital content were iPods and computers. Physical CDs and cassettes were in most people's vehicles, and a lot of people already owned those types of devices. With digital downloads and streams, you needed a digital player or had to burn CDs.

Digital media sales completely transformed the music recording industry once it took off in 2009. Over the years, digital music sales and digital streaming subscriptions have steadily grown, while physical music sales such as CD's and cassettes have declined for more than a decade. It is no surprise to see this evolution over time, as the music industry is known to be an ever-changing one.

The landscape of the music industry will continue to change and is likely to improve as long as technology keeps advancing alongside it. Music has transcended from being consumed through A-Tracks to being consumed through CDs, and today's music being consumed through music streaming services. CDs have become obsolete because music consumers either stream their music selections or purchase digital copies from digital retailers, which they can listen to on their smartphones or similar devices.

Summary on the Evolution of the Music Industry

1. The Live Music Industry Music Industry

We can conveniently state that as long as there were gatherings of people to watch people perform either for money or to be entertained, the Live Music Industry has always existed. As a musician, performing to an audience has continued from past times till date.

2. The Music Publishing Industry

With the invention of the basic printing press by Gutenburg for the church in the early 1600s, religious chant has been reproduced on paper. The industrial revolution in the 1800s gave music a better structure for delivery to a wider audience with the production of sheet (print) music. Composers could write their compositions on paper and deliver the same to hundreds of local orchestras who performed them.

3. The Recorded Music Industry

In 1877, Thomas Edison built on Leon Scott's first audio analysis invention (1857) that recorded on a piece of paper its audio input and created the machine called the phonograph. This tool could both record and playback audio recordings instantly using a thin metal cylinder. Different bands took advantage of the genius of Edison's invention resulting in the creation of the recording industry.

This period witnessed this recorded music industry focus more on the performer than the composers. The recording process became more sophisticated until Les Paul, in 1948, did the first multi-track recording. This eliminated the need for recordings to be taken live; it also paved the way for opportunities in artistic license.

Record labels brought together songwriters from the publishing industry and musicians from the live industry and created a vinyl for the recording industry that would hire people to scout upcoming artists.

4. Formation of the Music Industry

WW2 brought about significant improvements in communication technology; the music industry was not left out with these improvements. Many artists like Elvis Priestly, the Beatles, and Cliff Richard capitalized on them, delivering high-quality music for international audiences through record sales, live performances, and tours.

Wealthy individuals who saw the levels of record sales began to heavily invest in the industry, enabling merchandising, elaborate stage performances for promotion, the manufacture of large quantities of records that were distributed globally, and rewarding contracts for talented artists.

5. Technological Improvements

Compact tape cassettes came on the scene in the mid-1970s and CDs in the 1990s. The Internet was born in this period; its use expanded through the early 1990s, with individuals like Sean Parker, Shaun Fanning, and John Fanning creating Napster, a portal where people could download listed tracks. This development caused issues with intellectual property ownership resulting in the company getting sued and its eventual shutdown.

6. Reformations within the Music Industry

Sales of CD albums peaked in the early 2000s and began to decline as private individuals took to the Internet. Because the Internet lacks (and still lacks) intellectual property right laws, better still, international regulation, in their attempt to prevent revenue loss due to bootlegging, took many individuals to court. These litigations adversely affected publishing companies; they no longer had the resources necessary for their tours as a result of a lack of return on investment.

7. The Present and Future of the Music Industry

Today, the music industry is the largest it has ever been. Like in other years, it has changed its path to the market with numerous streams of income now available. Currently, recorded music sales are still the cash cow for the industry, with many companies transferring online via channels like eCommerce.

The Three Key Elements Driving the Evolution of Music and the Music Industry

1. Research

Figure Out Which Record Label

You must know the industry, know what you are doing; do it right, and be familiar with the best platforms available to do it on. Research is a key contributor to your success and longevity in this industry. You would agree that there was a steady scary decline in revenue generated by CDs from the 20th century till as late as 2018, indicating a massive fall within the CD industry. From 2018 onwards, digital platforms steadily grew, becoming the largest source of revenue within the music business.

These all show that the world of music is changing and you must have current and relevant information at your fingertips to be able to adjust and cope with the changes.

2. Content Production

In addition to research, you must know your product, develop it, nourish and refine it in the best way possible. As you grow as an artist, you must develop not just your music but your brand. Over the years, artists have been seen to collaborate with prominent photographers, dancers, videographers, and many more. They do this to improve their portfolio and how well they deliver the content they produce.

Today, YouTube is the most used music service. As an artist, this platform offers a great opportunity for you to create, upload, and share your music with the world. Several other platforms can help you create an alternate and unique voice for yourself. Using these services, you can blog, vlog, and even address some of the challenges you have faced within the industry. People want to know more than just the music you offer; you can also show the world more of your life as a musician.

3. Marketing

With advancements in technology, record companies and artists have increasingly used marketing vehicles such as *AI*, social media to reach potential customers, unlike previous years for promotions and service marketing.

Today, you can also harness these tools by:

- Posting your links on all your social media networks.

- Using the platforms to spend time with your fans via live chats.

- Collaborating with other artists and put yourself out there as much as possible.

Artists that Have Been Taken Advantage of by Major Record labels

Just a handful of people love accounting and its associated jargon, but the truth is that accounting is the language of Business. You may ask, "What does this have to with me getting robbed?" There is no denying that the music industry has been predatory over the years it has been in existence.

In this section, I will try to condense the stories as we look at some artists who were "robbed" by their record labels.

- **Michael Jackson**

Michael was a student of the game, the goings-on in the music industry. After numerous discussions with a figure like Paul McCartney, who schooled him on the importance of publishing, detailing his mishaps in the industry, the story does that MJ began to figure out ways to get into the business of publishing. He started buying everything and anything he could lay his hands on. His goal was to be the number one publisher in the world. Many people thought he was crazy.

Michael's sudden financial problems can be traced to the fact that he owned ATV Publishing (the Beatles Catalog). At the end of his contract, Sony offered him an irresistible offer. Michael got $18 million in advance for his album *Dangerous,* which sold more than $30 million worldwide. This was when his world began to crumble.

For the next decade, he was embroiled in controversies and legal matters. His problems made him take loans from *Sony,* who readily obliged. MJ eventually merged *ATV* and *Sony for* $115 million and got a stipend of $10 million.

His subsequent releases were not met with anything close to the fanfare and publicity of his previous albums, even though an album like *Invincible* had some bangers. Michael felt *Sony* had not done enough to promote this album and began to speak out. His many bold shots at Sony ruffled some feathers. He accused his record label of victimization and racism towards him because his success had surpassed anything they had imagined. He even went on to call Tommy Mottola, the then CEO of *Sony,* a devil.

By 2009, Michael Jackson was pronounced dead. In 2012, *Sony/ATV* announced that they would be the administrator of Michael's music with regard to his estate. When 2016 rolled around, *Sony* made an announcement that they would be acquiring the remaining half of Michael Jackson's *ATV's* Publishing for $750 million.

ATV (under *Sony*) spent three decades destroying Michael's life, his hard work and credibility, draining him of funds.

- **Prince**

The Purple One, as he was fondly known, didn't have the smoothest relationship with record labels. He famously compared a record contract to slavery, reflecting his drawn-out battle with Warner in 1993.

Prince signed with Warner Music in 1977 in his teens; his first album and subsequent albums from 1977 to 1981 were not high-scoring successes. He was kept on the label because Warner saw him as a musician who reflected well on the company and appeared in the public eye as a company committed to investing long term in serious talent.

In 1982, Prince released his next album, which peaked at the US billboard top 10 for the first time. As a result of his success alongside similar musicians of his caliber who understood the power of music videos, fans began to copy his look. By 1984, Prince became one of the biggest selling pop star globally.

Prince sought out to use his global success to get a fair record deal. In doing so, he set up his own label, Paisley Park Records, which was partly funded by Warner Brother Record Label (they also handled its distribution). In this capacity, he was responsible for scouting new talent and overseeing their artistic development. He released eight albums via Paisley Park/Warner from 1985 to 1992. This period marked an outstanding creative and commercial run in his life. However, this was going to be short-lived.

In the buildup to the release of his next album, The Golden Experience, Prince and Warner couldn't agree over both money and his music. He took this battle public by appearing with the word "Slave" written on the side of his face. Prince argued that the fact that he was signed to Warner meant that they owned and controlled his name as well as any music released under his name (sounds familiar?). These events coincided with George Michael's ill-fated attempt to part ways with Sony, which he termed "professional slavery." This meant that major record labels had a serious PR battle on their hands which they couldn't afford to lose because it would be bad for the whole recording industry if they lose. The Purple One had to fulfill the terms of his contract with Warner, which resulted in a rapid release of dismal albums.

The next two decades (1995-2014) marked a somewhat promiscuous run with various record labels. He released The Gold Experience under his new label New Power Generation (NPG); NPG/Warner. He eventually broke off the deal with Warner and signed a series of one-off deals with Warner's major rivals.

As a result of his journey through and with pretty much every major record label, his options were somewhat reduced. He eventually decided to release his albums himself online via various platforms.

- **Toni Braxton**

After several arduous weeks of renegotiating Toni Braxton's contract, it ended with Toni Braxton's lawyers filing a lawsuit against LaFace Records and Arista Records intending to declare Toni Braxton's contract no longer valid. Let's pause for a bit to get some background on her life and battle with LaFace/Arista Records since being signed to them in 1992.

Toni Braxton had burst onto the music scene in the '80s as of an R&B Quartet; The Braxtons formed with her sisters. However, with the successful release of her first solo single, "Love Shoulda Brought You Home," in 1992, she launched a solo singing career.

In 1996, Toni Braxton teamed up with R. Kelly, Babyface, Tony Rich, and David Foster on her album Secrets which she co-produced. It was a huge success. It peaked at number two on the Billboard, where it stayed for 92 weeks; it was nominated for Best Pop Album at the 1997 Grammys, where she bagged the awards for Best Female Pop Vocal Performance (Un-Break My Heart) and Best Female R&B Vocal Performance (You're Makin' Me High) as well as winning two American Music Awards, certified octuplet platinum. Secrets sold over 15 million copies worldwide, generating more than $170 million and further cementing her status as an international music superstar.

Toni Braxton generated millions for her record label Arista/LaFace. Despite the revenue Toni Braxton was raking in, she soon realized that she made less than 32 cents per album sold before paying back the record label recoupable cost spent on her creating and marketing her album. Toni Braxton was in a terrible financial mess. Toni Braxton eventually filed an unsuccessful lawsuit against the label. Eight weeks after filing the lawsuit, she filed for bankruptcy, which worked out in Toni Braxton's favor and allowed her to sign a new recording contract with Laface/Artista Records and get a multi-million dollar advancement on her future albums to be released on Laface/Artista Records.

Toni Braxton went on to reveal in various interviews that she had to file for bankruptcy due to the unfair recording contract she had with her label that amounted to her receiving less than $2,000 in royalties after paying back the label all recoupable costs and advancements taken against her album sale royalties. As a result of this, Toni Braxton had to reimburse her recording company for music video costs, clothes, travel, and studio time. In her words, "What happens is that they will give you an advance of a million on the next record and the next record, so you kind of stay in debt in a sense."

- **Mya**

In 1996, Mya signed a record deal with Interscope Records while she was still in high school as their first R&B female artist on their roster. Mya released her eponymous debut album, Mya, in 1998, which went platinum, and produced her first top ten single 'It's All About Me." Subsequent releases were successful and raised Mya's profile within the recording industry. Mya continued to rise to prominence in the music industry when she won her first Grammy Award in the category for Best Pop Collaboration with Vocals for her performance of Patti Labelle's "Lady Marmalade" with Pink, Christina Aguilera, and Lil 'Kim.

In July 2003, Mya released her third album Moodring. The album later went on to sell over 500,000 copies in the United States alone.

As Mya sought to take on a more active role in the production of her music, Mya soon discovered that Interscope was becoming primarily interested in being a rap/rock label, which caused Mya to switch record labels to release her future recordings.

Mya ended up signing a new recording contract with Motown Records to release her then untitled fourth album. Mya's release date of her fourth studio album Liberation was delayed and changed three times, which caused it to accidentally be released in Japan before proper promotion and marketing was done in order to bring awareness of the album being released. Mya's fourth album Liberation, eventually became available online for the bootleggers to download and file share, which caused the album to be shelved completely and never officially released in the United States. Mya decided against going to court to sue her record label "Motown Records" for the early leak of her fourth album "Liberation." When Mya's lawyer told her that the lawsuit could be a lengthy and expensive battle, Mya instead asked to be released from her recording contract with Motown Records, so she could have the freedom to sign with another label or go the independent route. Since Mya has often had struggles with her record labels Interscope and Motown records over artistic control, lack of promotion, and only netting 10 cents per album sold after repaying the record label back their recoupable costs and advancements, Mya chose to go the independent artist route moving forward.

Mya now releases her music on her own record label Planet 9 record label and is distributed through Tunecore. Mya has stated that she makes more money via independent route.

- **TLC**

The singing group TLC from Atlanta, Georgia who is composed of - Tionne "T-Boz" Watkins, Rozonda "Chilli" Thomas and Lisa "Left Eye" Lopes, owned the 90s with their brand of sizzling R&B hits. Their special delivery was smooth enough to win over millions, keeping them interested, and made them the most successful US girl group of all time. Their enormous level of success was supposed to keep them at the top of the charts, but it was cut short by the group's bankruptcy in 1995 and the tragic death of group member Lisa "Left Eye" Lopes on April 25th 2002. TLC fell victim to an unfair recording contract with Laface Records and Pebbletone Management (more on this later). The more you listen to their story, the more you realize it is another sad story of "Broke Artist versus Rich Label," a story that has been told repeatedly when young eager artists get the fame but not the fortune they were promised when signing their life away to a major record label.

Lisa "Left Eye" Lopes broke it down how TLC sold ten million copies of their sophomore album CrazySexyCool and be broke in a down-to-earth manner that anyone could understand; "There are 100 points on an album, TLC only received 7 of these points on their biggest selling album CrazySexyCool, every point is equal to 8 cents (7x8 = 56 cents). Every time an album gets sold, TLC gets 56 cents. 10 million (U.S sales) records equal $5.6 million dollars. This would be a decent amount of money if TLC did not have to pay to recouple cost back to the record label. The record company has spent around $3 million to record their album CrazySexyCool. In the record business, the artists pay all costs back to the record company. This includes pay recording costs, video costs and etc. So, TLC was left with $2.6 million. Which does not include the taxes of about 47.9%, which automatically gets deducted to $1.3 million, then you split the rest three ways." Not including them having to pay their lawyers, managers, and other personal expenses which left them each with around 200,000 dollars each.

This caused TLC to go bankrupt at the peak of its career. In the words of Watkins, "Everyone in this business has an agenda…people you think you know will keep running up the bill. You have to watch your back on every corner." You should study financial literacy and speak up for yourself. After TLC bankruptcy was over, they were able to receive new recording contracts that cut "Peppletone INC." completely out of the deal and got a 75 million dollar advance from Laface records. TLC was also able to obtain a new royalty rate of 18 percent versus their old rate of only 7 percent. TLC was one of the lucky artists that ended up getting a fair record deal after going to court and fighting for what was fair and due to them.

- **Destiny's Child**

La Tavia Robertson and LeToya Luckett of Destiny's Child filed suit against their former group members Kelly Rowland, Beyonce Knowles, and their manager Mathew Knowles for allegedly not informing them of being kicked out of Destiny's Child until they saw the music video for "Say My Name" with their replacements Farrah Franklin and Michelle Williams lip-syncing their parts in the video. The girls also claimed that they were not compensated fairly while in the group and their cell phones were being disconnected while Beyonce drove an expensive car. They also claimed they were not allowed to sing lead on the song because Mathew Knowles would tell the producers in the studio that only Beyonce "his daughter" is allowed to sing lead while Kelly Rowland "lived with the Knowles" could sing on the bridges or other smaller parts of the songs.

Letoya and La Tavia went on to sue the group's label, Sony Music, and every other party involved for breach of contract, defamation, libel, and fraud. They all reached a settlement of an undisclosed amount in 2002 and were released from any contracts they were signed to prior to giving them the freedom to sign with another label if they wished to.

- **Dixie Chicks**

The Dixie Chicks sued Sony Music Entertainment in July 2001. The Dixie Chicks has had a long-drawn-out dispute with Sony Music Entertainment that lasted for 11 months. The Dixie Chicks accused Sony Music Entertainment of "systematic thievery," cheating them out of over $4 million in royalties which they were owed for their first two multi-platinum albums. The Dixie Chicks also sought out to terminate the seven-year record deal they had signed with Sony Music Entertainment in 1997.

The trio (Emily Robson, Martie Seidel, and Natalie Maines Pasdar) has sold over 20 million albums that has generated more than $175 million for Sony Music Entertainment. In their words, "We refuse to sit back and silently endorse this behavior…a standard practice at Sony Music Entertainment…this is about people keeping their word." Sony in turn, counter-sued the group claiming they owed Sony Music Entertainment over $100 million for undelivered albums.

The Dixie Chicks later reconciled with Sony Music Entertainment and signed a new recording contract that gave the Dixie Chicks a $20 million bonus "non-recoupable payment or advancement against their future album royalties".

The Negative and Positive Effects of Technology on the Music Industry

The rare ability of music to speak to a person's soul in ways that resonate deeply with our emotions has made it stand the test of time. Just as humans are highly adaptive and has changed over time, so has music and all of the genres. Music has continually evolved regardless of the time and changes in the world. Human's innovation and ingenuity have brought on a powerful force that has impacted the music industry in remarkable ways throughout the years. The past two centuries have witnessed unprecedented technological advancements. Which have affected the way that music is produced, distributed, and accessed both in positive and negative ways.

Through the annals of history, technology has played a role in music but the most prominent has been the digitization of music, making it easier for artists to record, produce and release their music independently without the influence or help of major record companies. We have also seen how technology has reduced the cost of recording a project for artists since production equipment is now more durable and affordable.

With numerous digital platforms now available to indie artists, projects can now be released to digital retailers so they can easily be reached and accessed by the masses. Since the time music became readable by computers, the landscape, dynamics, and economy of the music industry have completely been transformed. Before this time, especially before the coming of digital retailers, it was difficult and nearly impossible for artists to get their CDs and cassettes across to retail stores for distribution if they were not signed to major record labels.

We will now take a look at how technology has impacted the music industry.

Pros

1. Better Production

The past two centuries have witnessed significant improvement in musical recording equipment and the emergence of new instruments that make music production and the recording process better than ever. For example, the twentieth century saw the emergence of one of the most influential methods of music production; the Synthesizer. The synthesizer is a product of the collaborative efforts of inventors and musicians who thought of ways of artificially reproducing the sounds of a plethora of musical instruments like the piano, drum, guitar, etc, by using electricity. Today, synthesizers have become a dominant feature in the instrumental niche and are commonly found on stage at major concerts as they produce sounds that were once the exclusive preserve of conventional instruments like the guitar and drum. Electronic music instruments continue to dominate music production and performances both on stage and in the studio so well that they have become key elements within countless genres like rock, country, and R&B that were once associated with traditional instruments. Computers have also made the production process easier to undertake in contrast to the old days when producers would spend long hours fine-tuning sounds on a complex analog device. Most of today's musicians can be seen working with samples and effects that are already on their computers and they alter these sounds to choose their preferred notes. Earlier musicians would have to think up their musical notes before they start working; this would require incredible thinking and writing prowess. Nowadays, musicians start with a raw idea and leverage the power of electronics to develop something valuable.

2. Improved Promotion

The advent of the Internet has made independent promotion more of a walk in the park than in the past. These days, with the click or the touch of a button, any good musician can be transformed into a global superstar. With file-sharing websites and social media, musicians can easily promote their projects and grow their space for more influence. Gone are the days when fans had to wait for the release of CDs, tapes, or some concert before they connect with their stars or experience the latest project of their idols.

3. Better Distribution/Sharing

In the old days, producing high-quality music was a herculean and difficult task. Rising through the ranks and breaking on the world scene was not for the lily-livered; it required significant effort and resources. As a result of logistical problems associated with the distribution of hard copies of musical projects, it took months and even years to be recognized as a musician worldwide. Nowadays, the story and landscape have changed in amazing ways thanks to advancements in technology and the Internet. Musicians can now get their music to a global audience without going through the rigors of transferring enormous volumes of hard copies to other regions of the world. Websites like Spotify and iTunes have provided platforms for artists to easily sell digital copies of their works just by the click of a button on a computer.

4. Accessibility

Today, your fans do not need to take long walks to a music shop to look for their favorite song. Right in the comfort of their houses or offices, they can now easily access the latest songs. The emergence of file-sharing sites has improved the way music is accessed. In less than 5 minutes, consumers can download the most recent songs, provided they have a good internet connection.

Cons

1. Music Piracy

Piracy has a negative impact on any artist or record label. Piracy has a negative impact on music streams and album sales. Piracy in layman's terms, is any form of theft; it is also the illegal use of a person's hard-earned talent – musical talent. Although piracy has been there since the 1920s, it took on a new turn with the invention of the mp3, which was basically marked the digitization of music. Thereon, it has been a massive struggle for the music industry to recover from the negative effects of bootlegging and illegal file-sharing. In 1999 before the World Wide Web blew up and became an enormous thing, music sales were at the peak. As a result of illegal file-sharing sites such as Napster and LimeWire, it caused a substantial slump in music sales since consumers now found it easy to download the works of musicians illegally for free and burn them onto CDs from the comfort of their homes.

This did a lot of damage to major record labels, so much that they began to reduce artist budgets earmarked to record and promote their new albums. Economic losses incurred with the music industry can easily be traced to Piracy as the main culprit. It equally changed the type of contracts that record labels offered artists; they took a piece of every revenue stream from the artists even though they do not provide assistance to the artist in earning that income. These new contracts are called 360 deals and were negatively received, with many well-established artists deciding to take the independent route because they saw this move as unfair and unjustified on the part of the record label. The decision by many of these established artists to go independent resulted in the creation of digital retailers like iTunes, Spotify, and Prime Music.

2009 marked the formation of the first music streaming company. It was a subscription-based music service that gave its subscribers access to more than fifty-five million songs for a monthly fee. In contrast to other ways customers got music, subscribers do not own any of the songs they download, and access to the music content will be lost once they stop subscribing to the streaming service.

2. Reduced Creativity as a Result of Over-reliance on Technology

While technology has significantly simplified a lot of the processes and reduced the effort required to producing quality music, overreliance on its benefits negatively impacts the quality of the music produced in the long run. These days, it is pretty difficult to come by musicians with pure originality, creativity, and the flair that makes music such an endearing and powerful force. Almost like football, the good old days had musicians who approached music as a calling and their sole passion. Even when the resources were limited, they delivered evergreen musical masterpieces that still resonate in our ears today. Even though they lacked swanky equipment to help them record and produce the kind of music we see today, they learned to appreciate music in its purest form. Music production and distribution are so simplified today that it has produced a lot of musicians who do not have any genuine purpose in music apart from the money and fame they crave. In clear terms, the music industry has suffered a loss of quality and character.

3. Undermining the Uniqueness of Cultures

Advancements in technology have made it possible for the world's cultures to share values, especially in music. The reality is that the more powerful cultures now dominate the scene and this results in other cultures assuming the values of the dominant ones. With today's technology, the sound from a particular dominant culture can be imposed on an artist's work because it is "exciting and cool." Some music genres from certain cultures are essentially dying as the younger generation and millennials start adopting the more popular ones. This is a genuine threat that undermines the diversity of the musical landscape. We would have a much better musical palette if new and indigenous forms of music are allowed to flourish while the older ones are still appreciated.

In summary, producing unique and valuable music is still not an easy task. But with the emergence of technology, the world of music has been transformed and improved in numerous ways. As technology keeps improving, the profession of music and the outlook of people will change accordingly. It's your duty as a player in the industry to find a way to let these two key elements, which are dear to us work hand-in-hand to progress and be distinguished out in the field. Although technology has both negatives and positives, music remains a major part of our lives, society, and cultures. We must work collaboratively to get rid of piracy for us to fully embrace the value of music and the musicians who work tirelessly to produce the songs we love.

CHAPTER 2
WHAT IS INDIE MUSIC?

It is difficult to say when indie music began. Generally, people believe that it started in the United States and the United Kingdom in the 1970s. This was a period the term became associated with independent artists/bands/labels and soon started to be used loosely to describe the genre.

The term "indie" derives from "independent" – a record label that operates independently from or without the support of mainstream record companies. Indie music comprises all music recorded and produced independently from commercial record labels or their affiliates through channels that may be described as an autonomous, do-it-yourself approach to recording, producing, and publishing. Indie music is known to have more grit and is less inclined towards commercial success.

An indie artist are not signed to any major record label. They are independent musicians or musical groups that are not under a contract with a major record label or any other similar company. These artists release music on their own record label or on an independent label record label; this means a record company unaffiliated with commercial, mainstream record companies "The Big Three Parent Record Labels." Terms associated with indie music are used in the music industry as a marketing technique. It's interesting to note that bands that publish their own projects on self-published CDs can also be termed unsigned bands.

Initially, artists who started out without being signed to a major record label usually sold their music and music-related merchandise independently while seeking a recording contract with a major record label by

Figure Out Which Record Label

sending their music to major record labels to try and get a deal. Today, artists use their social media accounts to post their music on or have popular social media influencers post their music on their social media accounts to get heard by their large following. There are also rare occasions when the music of indie artists are played on podcasts or radio stations targeting similar consumers. Some well-known artists who were once signed to major record labels such as Nine Inch Nails and Radiohead have started releasing their music independently. Others such as Beck and Oasis have risen from obscurity to AOR and Top 40 radio play without signing with a major label.

A handful of musicians remain independent and have become well known, while others started out as indie artists but later on get signed by a major record label and continue as a signed musicians. This concept has been changing in the past decade when major artists such as Mya, The Eagles, and Nine Inch Nails all decided to part ways with their major record labels such as Interscope Records and Universal Motown and remained successful without the support and backing of a major record label pushing their music. There are also artists like Chance the Rapper who has remained committed to the independent vision of releasing and promoting their own music. It is this kind of pacesetting independence that makes indie popular and influential.

Independent musicians have many services offered to them by which they retain the copyrights of their songs (masters) and also deliver their music to various online and off-site stores. As indie artists become more successful, it becomes more influential and inspiring to other artists who may want to take the leap of faith and go the indie route to release their music too.

When do Indie Artists Need a Manager?

When exactly do you know you're ready for representation?

Generally, it depends on the artist. There are many reasons artists may decide to get a manager on board to help them achieve their goals. You should typically begin searching for a manager when:

Figure Out Which Record Label

1. When your skillset is fully developed to a level where you have created your own brand – your look, your image, beat choices and sound.

2. When you can pull a large crowd at your local shows and events

3. When your daily task begins to become too overwhelming for you to handle yourself.

The reality is that managers can only do so much for you, depending on what you bring to the table. If you are not at a level where you can sell your records or tickets to your show, it may not be time for you to hire a manager.

If you have not released a project or two projects, you are probably not at a good place to hire a manager yet. As an artist who wants to thrive in the music industry, it is important for you to first make some music on your own. Produce a single and put it out there. If you have not done any live performances yet, you should work on doing that in order to have footage for a press kit in order to book other gigs.. There are a couple of reasons why you should do this;

1. It is proof to your manager that you're competent and committed to your music career.

2. You are truly independent, and you can make things happen on your own.

In some other cases, other artists may decide from the beginning to hire a manager to help them get their career off the ground. Whichever route you decide to take, as an indie artist, you need a manager who has your best interests at heart, one with a track record of success who is fearless and capable of helping you achieve your goals.

Yes, you could have your cousin or your friend as your manager even if this person may not have any experience in the artist management field. If they truly love your music and is passionate about it, they may even do better than conventional managers at pitching your music because they actually believe in you and the music that they are pitching.

As an artist, you must be true to yourself and also be authentic in order to build a loyal fanbase. If your manager does not want you to be yourself and understand this, they are probably not the right match for you. It is always imperative to remember that a manager can make your career a successful one and a bad one can ruin your career before it takes off.

It is also important to remember that there are different types of managers artists can choose from depending on the artists' personal situation and what their needs are from their manager. Artists do not need every type of management that the entertainment has to offer them. This is why I advise that the artists who are just starting out not to sign a long-term contract with any manager. A one-year management contract with options will be enough for you and your manager to feel each other out.

Typically, managers are the ones to present you with a contract. Some artists just need consultation. If you think that you can use advice from your consultant to take your music to the next level, I personally think that watching them transform into your manager wouldn't be a difficult process. Keep in mind that managers aren't paid by the hour; they are paid commissions from whatever the artists receive. In this way, they are fully aligned with you as an independent artist.

Many indie artists do not think they need a manager at the beginning of their career; they consider hiring one an inconvenience and unimportant. You need a manager; that will play essential role in your artist development. Competent managers help you fully concentrate on creating quality music while they deal with the rest of the process, like setting up bookings and organizing the rest of your team.

Your management team determines your long-term growth and success as an artist. They should be able to help you organize the business side of things; set up PR campaigns to make you visible on media platforms.

I will therefore advise that you examine your management team carefully and settle on one that you feel best suits your needs. Make sure they are familiar with the local scene and can help you achieve your goals.

Pros and Cons of Being an Indie Artist

Some artists choose to switch from an independent label to a mainstream label when presented with the opportunity because major labels are known to have more power and have more resources to promote and execute musical projects, hence increasing their chances of more success. In contrast, other artists may decide to remain independent instead of going to a major label if given the opportunity because independence generally gives them more freedom to create the music they want and promote it the way they feel fit.

Some others may become indie artists after spending some time recording on a mainstream, commercial label. A musician like Bradley Joseph asked to be let go from his contract with a major label, Narada/Virgin Records. He subsequently became an independent artist. He once said, "As an independent, business is a prime concern and can take over if not controlled. A lot of musicians don't learn the business. You just have to be well-rounded in both areas. You have to understand publishing. You have to understand how you make money, what's in demand, and what helps you make the most out of your talent. But some artists just want to be involved in the music and don't like the added problems or have the personality to work with both". Joseph clearly suggests that it's important that new artists take some time to study and understand both sides to music production before settling down on the one that best meets their needs and aspirations.

Successful independent labels with a strong musical reputation are influential and can be very appealing to major recording companies. They often look to independent labels to stay current with the ever-evolving music industry.

When musicians who were once signed to an independent label move to a major label, they are offered better opportunities for success but aren't always guaranteed success. Just one in ten albums released by major recording companies is regarded as a success or makes a profit.

Some indie artists have recorded for independent record labels the entire length of their careers and have gone on to build solid careers. Independent record labels are usually barometers of musical ingenuity and authenticity because their artists are allowed to be more creative and retain control over their music. However, independent labels that are creative and productive are not always financially lucrative. They are often managed by one, two, or only half a dozen people, with almost no external support with their business run from relatively tiny offices.

It is this lack of resources that make it difficult for artists to generate revenue from music sales. In many ways, it also makes it difficult for the indie label to get its artists' music aired on radio stations when compared to the pull of a major record label. The fact that since 1991, only twelve independent label albums have peaked at number one on the US *Billboard* 200 Album Chart is a testament to this. This is not to say other indie albums have not achieved relative success - tons of independent albums have reached the top 40 of the Billboard 200.

Today, many artists use their own resources to record, produce, market and release music via streaming platforms like Spotify, SoundCloud, and various social media networks in a direct, hands-on manner allowing creative distribution.

The majority of major record label artists only receives between 10–18% royalty rate for their album and music streaming sales. But, before an artist or band receives any of their album or streaming sales royalties, they must offset all the debt "recoupable costs" they owe their record label. This debt is known as recoupable expenses/costs. They arise from the cost of such things as video production, album packaging, costume, artwork, and tour support. Additionally, part of the recoupable expenses includes the artist's advance, which is very much like a loan given by the label record to the artist.

This advance allows the artist to have cash-in-hand to live and record with until their record is released. Nonetheless, before they can be paid any royalties, the advance must be repaid in full to the record company. It's noteworthy that only the most successful artists recoup production and marketing costs. In some cases, depending on the contract that the artist signed the debt of an unsuccessful music project might carry over to their next album, which can result in them not receiving any royalties payments for that albums sales or streams either, which continues to leave the artists in debt with their record label.

Advances from major record labels are usually larger than those offered by independent record labels. Let's say a major record label offers their artist an advancement in the range of $150,000–$500,000; smaller independent record labels may not offer the artist an advancement at all; they would just front the artist recording cost, traveling, features, artwork, and album packaging, and etc. These expenses would also be a recoupable expense that had to be paid back to the label record before the artist began to receive royalties from album sales and streaming revenue. When artists are not offered or do not take any advancements from the record label, the artist owes their record label less money which will allow the artist to start receiving royalty checks from the album and streaming sales earlier in situations where album sales and streaming revenue are good enough to warrant a return to the artist.

Since the record label generally recoups numerous costs of the album by receiving their share and keeping the artists' album sales and streaming revenue royalties until all recoupable costs are paid back to the record label in full, A lot of artists feel that they should get a large advancement from the major record labels since they may not receive royalty checks from their album and streaming sales for a long time; depending on how much revenue the artist's album generates. An advancement also puts the artist at an advantage because the advancement money owed by the artist is only recoupable through the artist's royalties, not through the artist other revenue streams. This shows that the priorities for independent artists and those signed to major labels are quite different.

Independent record labels contracts are not overly different from those offered by major labels because they have similar legal obligations that define how artists will be represented. However, there are slight differences in relation to smaller advances, reduced studio costs, and larger royalty rates, but also offers artists a fewer number of album options that the record label can choose to exercise. As a result of financial limitations, indie artists usually have less money to spend on marketing and promotion than artists signed to major labels. But with a larger royalty spilt, lower production and promotion costs, independent record labels can easily make a profit from selling a lot less albums than a major record label can.

There have been instances of profit-sharing deals with an independent label in which an artist receives as much as 40–50% of the net profits. This type of contract implies that the net gain after all deductions have

Figure Out Which Record Label

been made is divided between the label and acts at a pre-determined percentage. However, in such deals, the artist may have to wait for a lengthy period to gain any profits, if at all, because you must take into account all expenses – such as hotels, tours, recording, manufacturing, music videos, publicity, and marketing, etc. The only way this type of deal benefits an independent artist is if they become very popular. We have a closer look at this type of deal in Chapter 3.

Independent record labels do not have as many connections as a major record label does, so they rely heavily on personal networking, or "word of mouth", to gain visibility and get their music out there and talked about by the masses. Independent record labels naturally avoid all forms of high-budget marketing tactics because of their financial constraints. This, in the long haul, helps to lower production costs and may help fast-track the record label and the artists to receive payment of their royalties sooner, if warranted. Major record labels typically have their eyes on artists on independent labels because they are able to measure their prior success, and if the major record label is interested in the artist, they may offer them a record contract with their record label when the artist old contract with the indie record label is up. In some instances, if the major record label is extremely interested in the indie artists, they may offer to buy them out of their current contract with the indie record label. If this occurs, then the major record label may pay the independent record label a substantial payment in order to get them to sell the contract to them. The volume of sales of Independent music is difficult to track. As a result of this, many of them miss out on payments they should receive as royalties. In the music world, song credits and all underlying information tied to a released song you see on streaming services like Apple Music or Spotify needs to be synchronized across every industry database to ensure that when a song is played, the relevant people are identified and paid. This doesn't always happen. As a result of these inconsistencies, billions are left on the table that never gets paid to indie artists who earned that money.

The Internet has been creatively and profoundly used by many indie artists to gain popularity with their fans and to break into the mainstream charts. Resources on the Internet are now being harnessed to promote, market, and sell their music almost free of charge.

Indie artists can now upload their songs and lyrics to underground music sites like Vimeo Music Store and Radio Reddit and have them rated and promoted on unsigned charts. Many domain owners of these sites have spent substantial amounts of money developing these charts to make them appealing to the artists. A number of these charts are now registered on official music charts.

Blogs have also become a popular way indie artists get their music into the ears of the right people in the industry. Blogs often offer emerging artists the opportunity to be interviewed, have their EP reviewed and added to playlists. Others provide helpful guidance, wide-ranging leadership, and resources for new indie artists of all genres.

Tips to Building Your Team as an Indie Musician

There comes a time for every artist to decide to transition from taking music as a hobby to making it an actual career and earning a living for themselves. As we find in all industries, the success of an independent artist largely depends on the team they have supporting them. We have already considered when an indie artist needs a manager; we will now look at when and how to effectively build a team backed with the knowledge that the size and composition of each team vary from artist to artist.

Here are some things you must know before building your team:

1. Work with people who believe in you and are passionate about your success

For your career to be successful, your team members must be on the same page with you and should be as excited as you are about what you do even if you had the best publicist, the most connected manager, and an experienced agent if they do not believe in your music or you as an artist, your career will not be as successful as it could be if they did. A friend who is passionate about your career and is keen on seeing you succeed can take you further than a host of professionals who do not believe in you.

2. Pace yourself and Set your goals

Figure Out Which Record Label

It makes a whole lot of sense to co-opt new members into your team as more needs arise than having the entire team at a go. Be sure of your short-term and long-term goals, and know where you need assistance. As a performing artist, some signs that you are struggling and need the help of more experienced hands are when you have many requests coming in; you can't keep up with the business and logistics of your career, you want your career to take a different direction because you want to reach a wider audience with your music, or you want to focus on performing rather than the business side of the licensing and distribution of your projects.

Generally, it's advisable to gradually build your team and only bring new hands-on board as your needs increase and your goals expand. Once you have the right people on your team and you all have a clear understanding of what you want to accomplish, meeting your goals will be easier.

We will now have a breakdown of the key players you should have in mind as you build your team and when it might be time to hire them, their job description, and how they are usually compensated.

1. Manager

We have comprehensively covered this base in a previous section:

2. Marketing Companies

Getting your music on the airwaves and getting some traction is the dream of every artist, marketing companies are well equipped to help you accomplish this. There is really no specific time to bring on a marketing professional or team if you can afford it. As long you have a new high-quality release ready to hand over to the marketing company.

A marketing company will help you with creative strategies, whether paid or organic to promote your work and execute your projects. They will provide you with valuable insights into your audience and ways to leverage such information. They should give weekly reports.

The remuneration for marketers is typically fee or percentage-based. When it is fee-based, it will be a monthly fee for a fixed number of months. Percentage-based payments, on the other hand, are made as a percentage of the total ad spend; for example, you set aside $3000 for a Facebook ad, the firm will take $300 and spends the other $2700 on the ad. Fee-based ads make the most sense for smaller budgets and emerging artists.

3. Publicists

Like the marketing company, a publicity firm or publicist can be brought on when you have an album release or a worthwhile project on the horizon. Publicists usually work on a sound recording, an album, a single track, tours, and other notable events. Before bringing them on, you must have generated some buzz online or with the press that they can work with.

The least you should expect is a three-month commitment. The work of the publicist entails building your story and pitch, so they will need some time to accomplish this. Anything less than three months will not be enough for them to achieve this. PR campaigns are usually tough to predict, so it's best to keep your expectations in check. Your PR should give you regular reports, ensure they do this, so you are able to monitor their work results.

Publicists (independent or firms) work on a retainer basis, and you should agree in advance to commit a certain length of time. They can run PR campaigns from $500 - $1000 per month or $10,000 upwards per month.

4. Booking Agents

You should bring in a booking agent when you start making steady earnings from your work – this is preferable. You don't need to overwork yourself, be focused, and build your profile; they will surely come looking for you.

Your management will work closely with your booking agent to book slots, events and shows a minimum of 4 – 5 months out. While making good music, building and enhancing your profile, inform your manager/agent when you get a new connection for them to fix you up.

Agents like managers take a commission of the top of your shows and average about 10%.

5. Labels or Independent Distribution

Figure Out Which Record Label

There comes a time when signing with a label makes sense, similar to management. When you start making strong record sales, you'll know it's time to seek out a record deal or find distribution support for your new projects. If you have been approached by a label for a deal that looks promising, ensure you have an experienced attorney review the deal before you make any move to sign. If you choose to review the deal on your own, do this with caution, read between the lines and ensure you know 100% the terms and conditions of the deal to avoid getting your fingers burned.

Your expectation from a deal largely depends on the circumstances and the size of the label; is it a small independent label or an established label? Generally, you should expect regular communication, thorough planning, and solid support from the label. If this is not happening, it might be time to consider your options and look elsewhere.

Record label gets paid a percentage of your income from record sales. There are certain contracts where the label will own your masters and publishing forever or for a period of time; others will vary. Labels typically give advances to their artists which will be paid back in full from the artist's album and streaming royalties.

6. Publishers or Sync Licensing Teams

As soon as you own a solid catalog of records or you have released projects with other artists, it might just be time to hire a publisher. There are many publishing deals.

Publishers will help manage your music catalog and take you to the next level – giving you more visibility in the industry. They can facilitate collaborations with other artists and pitch your music to labels, more established artists, and music supervisors for placements in film, TV, mobile apps, video games, and advertising. Publishing deals can be full-on publishing deals where communication between the artist and publisher happens either on a daily or weekly basis. For non-exclusive sync deals, communication is usually occasional, mostly when the artist has a new project to share or when/if the publisher has an offer for the artist.

A publisher will be paid a percentage of the artist's income. Sync deals normally range from 20 – 30% of all sync licenses, this percentage can be as high as 50% in a non-exclusive deal.

7. Tour Management and Other Tour Support Personnel

Tour managers and support personnel should be hired when you have a substantial number of tour dates and you a guaranteed sum of money that can adequately cater for your staff.

Experienced tour managers will advance your shows a month or two before the tour kicks off. They will collect and communicate all the details needed for all the shows, make arrangements for accommodation, travel, venue, daily meals, and everything else the band will need to make the tour a success. A tour manager must be reliable and trustworthy.

The tour staff normally receive a flat fee per show, per day, or per tour.

8. Promoters

You should bring a promoter on board when you have a new recording and you are going on tour. It's usually a great time to hire a promoter when you have a new release and you are planning a tour. Although promoters and publicists may sound like professionals doing the same job to the layman, their tasks are remarkably different. Promoters use every possible avenue to promote your music; radio, social media. It's good to have promoters informed of tour dates throughout the campaign.

Promoters should always be kept in the loop with all your projects that can help their pitching drive, so it's better to plan a campaign some months in advance of a release/tour and for the campaign to exceed a month or more. During an ongoing campaign, expect your promoter to deliver weekly reports regarding opportunities they have pitched for.

Promoters normally charge a flat fee for each campaign. Their charge depends on the number of formats that they are working on. Some other promoters like radio promoters will charge a "life of record" fee, this means that they will keep the record on their roster indefinitely and pitch it for opportunities and respond to inquiries as they come up.

Successful Indie Artists

In those days, getting signed to a major label meant you had made it and hit stardom. Today, things have changed, many musicians do not know what to expect because mainstream labels are fast losing their position to independent musicians. To make things even worse, there have been reports of major record labels ripping off artists signed to their labels, bullying and extorting creatives.

The path provided by indie artists leads to remarkable experiences in which different creative people from various backgrounds, with different skillsets and expertise, collaborate to produce music that is unique, diverse, and resonates with an equally diverse audience. The indie route allows for self-expression and creative control that rarely happens working under a major record label. This is the overriding reason musical acts work hard to develop the organic awareness needed to make an indie release succeed and to protect the freedom that follows. By networking and working collaboratively with their own supportive communities, indie artists go on to succeed.

In the 21st century, in which we find ourselves, there are really no significant differences between a major record label release and one from a big independent record label. Sure, major labels may still give their artists bigger bonuses and better backing, but many of today's top artists are glad to sacrifice such large advancements for creative control. Part of the appeal for many indie artists is that this path encourages experimentation; they can draw from different fields and take chances as they deem fit. Some others like Chance the Rapper, turned down advancements from a major record label for the opportunity to work with whomever they choose at their own pace and his creative freedom when creating his music.

Notable artists who either left their major record labels or refused to model themselves to the major record label include Chance the Rapper, White Mystery, Nipsey Hussle, Ashanti, Macklemore, Frank Ocean, TI, Noname, Iggy Azalea, David Choi, and Thundercat. Let's examine some of these indie artists.

1. Chance the Rapper

Figure Out Which Record Label

Back in 2013, Chancellor Bennett (a.k.a. Chance the Rapper) released his Acid Rap mixtape; he could easily have ridden the waves of its success and signed with any of the major labels. Instead, he decided to forgo labels entirely and moved to Los Angeles to produce good music with some of his friends in the band the "Social Experiment."

In a 2015 interview with *The Fader,* he said, "I've met with every A&R, VP of A&R, president of the labels, CEOs. I know all these people." He turned down all of them. Today, he loves his freedom as an artist. This is one of the things you pay in exchange for a record deal. The takeaway here is that if you are talented, you know what you are doing and you are willing to learn the business side of the music industry, you don't need to sign with a major record label at all. Chance the Rapper has earned himself seven Grammy Award nominations and won three without the help of a major record label, and Chance the Rapper is only going to get bigger and better as he continues on his journey within the music industry.

2. Iggy Azalea

In 2018, Iggy Azalea left her former record label Island Def Jam Records to sign a multi-million distribution deal with Empire Records and created her own record label Bad Dream Records where she has total creative control over her musical and aesthetic direction and retains ownership of her masters in addition to a 50/50 profit split with Empire Records.

3. Frank Ocean

In 2016, Frank Ocean split from Def Jam in order to take the independent route. Forbes projected that Frank Ocean's move from a major record label to an indie route may have more than doubled his profit for the release of his album *Blonde*. Frank Ocean is no newbie. Frank Ocean knows his numbers; in an interview with the New York Times, Frank Ocean said, "I need to know how many records I've sold, how many album equivalents from streaming, which territories are playing my music more than others, because it helps me in conversations about where we're gonna be playing shows, or where I might open a retail location, like a pop-store or something." Today, Frank Ocean is a leading voice and championing the change for Indies. Frank Ocean is a prime example of the type of business savvy that indie artists who desire relevance and success must foster.

4. Ashanti

Ashanti decided to take the independent route when she formed her own record label, Written Entertainment, through a joint venture deal with E1 Music, one of the world's biggest independent distribution companies. Ashanti now retains ownership of all her masters and has the creative freedom to do whatever she wants creatively.

5. Jean Weaver

Jean Weaver and her band signed a recording contract with Polydor Records in the early '90s. When Jean Weaver and her band was taking advantage of by their A&R, who told Jean Weaver that their new album they had invested so much effort and time in for months would not be released unless Jean Weaver and her band was willing to take a huge pay cut for their unreleased album. Jean Weaver and her band then decided to go the indie route. Although Jean Weaver and her band battled with financial restrictions to finish their album "*The Silver Globe* album, being an independent artist allowed her to experiment and to make it happen on their terms without restrictions from a record label.

6. TI

American Rapper TI also chose to go independent after a failed record deal with Columbia Records in 2018. Today, he releases music through his own record label Grand Hustle.

7. Thundercat (Stephen Bruner)

Thundercat is one of the music industry's most talented bassists. Thundercat has worked with some of the industry's most talented artists, such as Kendrick Lamar and Michael Donald. Thundercat has successfully released three albums, all through his collaboration with Flying Lotus' independent label.

CHAPTER 3
PROS AND CONS OF SIGNING WITH MAJOR RECORD LABELS

Different Types of Recording Contracts

There are several different record deals that record companies can offer to artists and other labels. These deals often change based on the direction of the industry. In recent times, most record deals have been in favor of artists, especially if they have a large fan base, track of success within the record industry, and the current amount of hype that the artists currently have.

Recording contracts can be broken down into two types; one where the labels own the rights to an artist's recordings and the other where the artist owns the rights of their original recordings (master copyright). Recording contracts only cover the recordings of an artist and are separate from publishing contracts. They can vary depending on the specific type of deal, but generally, they are several similarities.

Standard Record Deal

Unlike the name suggests, the SRD is focused largely on albums and options and is an offer that was more suited to the analog age than the digital era of today.

Since recording contracts come in different shapes and sizes and often vary depending on the label and status of the artist, they can be quite hard to understand. Broadly speaking, their commercial terms are often similar; hence, they require closer inspection to decipher.

Recording contracts are legally binding agreements that enable record labels to generate revenue by exploiting the musical projects and careers of an artist.

This is achieved through the physical sale of records, live performance, broadcasting of musical works, and the sale of digital products such as downloads, video games, and mobile ringtones.

The recording contract defines a record to include audio-visual devices and other new technologies caught by this definition. In a recording contract, the artist is obligated to sign to the label exclusively. This implies that they cannot record for another label without permission; neither can they terminate the contract before it ends without fulfilling the terms stipulated in the contract for a termination. The record label, however, has the prerogative to sign, promote and build the career of as many artists as it desires.

Record labels usually demand huge sums of money to terminating an artist contract and claim that they need this level of control over an artist to improve the chances of making a profit or to cut their losses. There are a few occasions where artists get one over on the label. In terminating her long-term contract with EMI in 2002, Mariah Carey called her decision "the right decision for me." This may not be unconnected with the $28 million EMI had to pay her to end the contract early after her public breakdown in the media in 2002.

Territory

Artists that are normally signed to a record label are usually signed to a deal that covers all the territories worldwide. Most mainstream recording companies like Sony/BMG, Universal, and Warner have offices in all the major markets around the world, and so they have a wide distribution network capable of delivering their latest projects worldwide. Split-territory deals are not common with major record labels because they have the connections and abilities to push their artists' music worldwide. Independent record labels on the other hand, may be more willing to agree to such an arrangement since they do not have the same resources as a major record label.

Term and Options

This defines the duration of the contract. It is usually calculated using an initial fixed period as reference, for instance, 12 months when an artist makes their first album, followed by further option periods, also usually of 12 months, allowing the record company to extend the deal if they wish. A minimum commitment within each period will also be stipulated, requiring artists to deliver a specific number of tracks under the label, with a total of about five to six albums is standard in today's recording contract.

Options do not mean that the label is committed to recording more albums with the artist; they basically mean that the label has the option to record more if the label choices too. The record label binds the artist more than they bind themselves to the artist. With this in place, an artist will always want to commit to the fewest options possible when negotiating their recording contract. This will allow the artist more flexibility and bargaining power in the long term with their record label. From the label's viewpoint, options also give them some flexibility in their working relationship with the artist if their projects show the record's chart potential. They will also want to avoid a situation where an artist decides to move on to another major label after they have invested time, effort, and resources into an artist's career to help them achieve some recognition in the marketplace. It is advisable to negotiate a 'long-stop provision' so that the entire duration of the contract doesn't exceed a maximum of seven years.

Rights Granted

Recording contracts are typically exclusive, meaning that the artists do not own their masters and the record label does. This is a transfer of ownership for the full life of the copyright. It is usually 50 years from the date of release for sound recordings.

Many artists signed such deals in the past. Taylor Swift, who is probably the most successful solo pop artist of the past decade, announced a new deal with Republic Records in November 2018 and left Big Machine. Taylor Swift's deal with Big Machine, which she signed when she was 15, stipulated that her master copyrights were owned by the label and its owner, Scott Borchetta. Attempts to make a copy of her master recording in any form would require the approval of the owner of the rights and the payment of a fee. In June 2019, Scooter Braun, who Swift had accused of "bullying" bought Big Machine. This meant that he now owned her masters. Taylor Swift ended up leaving Big Machine Records and signed a new deal with Republic Records, where Taylor Swift will now own all of her masters of the album she releases under them. Taylor Swift also found a cause in her contract that allows her to rerecord her previously released albums under Big Machine Records after a certain amount of years passed, which would allow her to own her own set of masters of her first 6 studio albums.

Simply Red's Mick Hucknall is another musician who had a run-in with his former record label, Warner Bros Music. Mick Hucknall made millions ($192 million) of dollars for Warner Bros Music but still had no access to the masters of his own music. Mick Hucknall parted ways with the company back in 2000 to go the indie route and release music through his own record label and website simplyred.com, claiming the deal with Warner was "immoral."

Some issues must be taken note of here; firstly, the artist's unreleased recordings are owned by the label throughout the artist's career. Secondly, even when the label has received recoupable costs from the artist, they still own the masters. These are some of the reasons many musicians choose to terminate their contracts, especially when their labels refuse to renegotiate the terms of the contract.

There are rare cases where an artist succeeds in securing a reversion of the copyright clause in their contract, allowing them the return of their masters at a future date. Robbie Williams' had such a trailblazing deal with EMI in 2002, which granted him such rights. The reality is that few artists can pull such a deal.

Labels may also decide to acquire the rights to the album artwork, the artist's name, and the image used to sell and promote the records.

Release Commitment

The goal of the artist should be to secure a fair recording contract from the record label that includes a reasonable financial commitment to support the artist's music released on the label and a fair release commitment cause for the artist. An artist should be able to terminate a contract and/or buy back their recordings if the label fails to release their record. This is the role a release commitment fulfills in a recording contract.

Key-man Provision

What will you do if the manager who signed you suddenly leaves the label, or your A&R is shady like in the Jane Weaver example from earlier in the book? Situations like these can be avoided when you negotiate a key-man clause in your recording contract. This provision also allows you to leave the record label, which would then allow the artist to sign with a different record label without any negative penalties instead of being left at a record label where no one believes in them or knows how to market them.

Advancements

Advancements are upfront payments from the record label to the artist taking into consideration future royalties; meaning that it is an investment that the label expects to recoup from the artist. These sums are paid to the artist when the artist signs to the record label and again as and when further options in the contract are exercised. Artists usually don't receive any royalties until the record label has fully recouped the advancements it paid to the artist.

It is advisable for artists to negotiate a generous advancements to exercise successive options in the artist recording contract, ie, at the release of the next album regardless of whether previous advancements have been fully recouped. While preparing contracts, a lot of care should be taken to expunge any wording that presents an advancement as repayable. Such a statement would have the knock-on effect of turning an advancement into personal debt, which the artist could be liable for at any time. Artists should only have to repay advancements from income that was generated through record sales. If the artist does not generate enough record sales for the record label to be able to fully recoup all the artist expenses and advancements paid to them; then the record label has to bear that loss when this occurs.

Large or generous advancements are useful for the artist, especially when an artist has to split the advancement with various members of their team or group members.

Recording Costs

Artist advancements are usually meant to be used for the recording cost of the album and funds for the artist to live off of. From the advancement funds, a specific amount is allocated to the recording budget, with any surplus going into the account of the artist. It is good practice for the artist to apply intelligence and spend wisely because the full amount of the advancement is recoupable from their royalties. If the artists does not handle their advancement funds properly, the artist could end of with nothing and will not receive any more payments from the record label until all of the artist expenses is fully recouped.

Like I pointed out early, artist managers are usually paid a commission between 10-20%. The artist must ensure that the manager only receives commission on the non-recording portion of the advancement fund specifically, what's left over after the recording budget has been agreed upon.

Royalties

Royalties are paid to artists based on record sales and music streaming revenue. In a typical major record label recording contract, the artist will be paid between 12-18% of the record's wholesale price. But before the artist can receive any of these funds, recording costs, video costs (usually 50% is the artist share that has to be repaid back to the label), and the artist advancements will have to be recouped by the record label. Other deductions may also be made by the record label, further reducing the real royalty rate that the artist receives. These deductions are called eStandard deductions, usually include a packaging deduction of 20 to 25 percent on CDs, a reduced royalty rate on foreign album sales and streaming revenue and video albums, budget records "discounted albums", and CD's clubs, and most of the time the artist does not receive royalties on free goods such as records given away to digital retailers and the media. It is done this way because the artists only generate an income from royalty-bearing album sales records.

It is also noteworthy that artists might only get paid on 90 percent of their actual sales because retailers can return records they do not sell back to the record label. As a result of this, the record label may choose to withhold some of the artist's royalties as a reserve until all sales are verified. Artists must therefore ensure that this reserve is paid out regularly, and they are paid their full entitlement.

What we often find is that 'deductions' are artificial and do not always reflect exact costs to the label. This can be seen in the cheap cost of the packaging of CDs manufactured in bulk. Today, with more records sold through digital channels, a reserve for damaged records, and allocations of free digital goods no longer make sense, all of these simply boost the label's profits.

Producer Royalty

Artists are expected to compensate the producer's royalties from their own royalty share. For instance, if a producer is paid a 4 percent royalty rate and the artist royalty rate is 20 percent, the artist will end up with an actual royalty rate of 16 percent after the deductions. Keep in mind that the artist will still pay their manager a commission and the other members of their team. In the case of the producer, they will comfortably earn 4 percent from the very first album sold.

The record label is allowed to recoup from the artist's royalty-income advancements that were paid directly to the producer. In some countries, the label is responsible for producer advancements. Also, the artist can negotiate with their record label to have the producers 4 percent from their royalty share and the artist. In some case, the artists negotiate for the record label to split the producer 4 percent royalty rate 50/50, which would also allow for the artist to keep a higher percent of their album sale royalties.

Secondary Income

A well-negotiated deal normally ensures that the artist receives 50% of all secondary income earned by the label.

Promotion and Tour Support

Promotion involves raising the profile of a new release by getting the artist to undertake some domestic and international promotional work. This can be done via different media channels. Some artists promote their projects by webcasting their tours; others receive support from their record labels via radio, press, and other various media platforms. Regardless of the approach taken to promote a new release, these costs can add up fast and it is important for the artist to negotiate some tour support from their record label in their recording contracts to help offset some of these costs to the artist.

Costs incurred for tour support are usually recoupable by the record label unless negotiated in the artist recording contract. Therefore it is imperative for the artist to come to a pre-determined spending limit before executing the actual tour promotions. It is not uncommon for the record label to budge and agree to help the artist with some type of tour support rather if it's a set dollar amount or agreeing to only take 50 percent of the total tour support cost recoupable against the artist album sale royalties and music streaming revenue.

Other terms of importance in a recording contract include warranties, grounds for termination, recording restrictions, controlled compositions, accounting, and dispute resolution.

Pros and Cons of 360 Deals

A 360 deal is a recording contract between an artist and a record label in which the record label agrees to provide financial and other types of support for the artist. In turn, the artist agrees to give the record label a part of the artist different revenue streams.

This recording contract is an alternative to the traditional recording contract. In a 360 recording contracts, a major record label "sometimes" provides support to artists in additional areas in the entertainment industry that are not covered in a traditional recording contract on the condition of receiving a percentage of revenue from these areas. In the early part of the 21st century, revenues and profit margins from released music has declined dramatically. Hence, the 360 recording contract shows that a significant amount of an artist's income is generated from sources beyond recorded music sales and licensing, such as tours, live performances, endorsements, book deals, and merchandise, "just to name a few."

The 360 recording contract is usually between 3 – 7 years and 5 – 7 years. With this recording contract, the artist gives up a percentage of their income (royalties, show money, ancillary income like merch, publishing, touring, fan club, etc.)

There are usually two components in a 360 Deal:

1. The first part covers record sales and music streaming; its terms are basically the same as those of a traditional recording contact with the artist being paid on a "royalty rate" basis;

2. In the second part, the record label is given the right to receive a percentage from other sources of income such as publishing, touring and merch which labels have not historically shared in. "or in most cases, the record company did not assist the artist in making this revenue."

360 recording contracts do not have a standard. Back in the early 2000s, 360 recording contracts were 50/50 splits except for show money which was a 30/70 split. The terms of these recording contracts vary substantially, and from record label to record label, and largely depend on how much the artist receives as an advancement from the record label, their profile, and

negotiating leverage "social media following, music streams, Youtube views, and the artists overall brand."

There are many variations to 360 recording contract; a "full" 360 recording contract empowers the record label to be paid a percentage of all related entertainment industry income, including touring, merchandising, endorsements, and publishing income, and so on. Many 360 recording contracts are not "full" 360 recording contracts; in which the record label only shares in specific types of the artists' income streams, such as touring and merchandising.

The record label's share of non-record kinds of income streams is commonly in the range of 10 to 20 percent, but for new artists, it's usually higher and can get as high as 50 percent.

Many musicians, such as Robbie Williams (with EMI in 2002), have made 360 recording contracts with traditional record labels. Others 360 recording contract deals have been made between artists and promoters such as that of Madonna and Jay-Z with Live Nation in 2007 and 2008, respectively.

The general decline in music revenue from physical music sales throughout the last decade has prompted numerous music distributors to enter into more robust and far-reaching arrangements with the artist they sign. Today, recording contracts are now more elaborate transcending, unlike the traditional recording deals, which solely involved a recording agreement. These new 360 recording contracts are often now referred to as "multiple rights deals" and are sometimes also called "360^0 deals," "270^0 deals," or "'180^0 deals," depending on the rights that are contracted for.

Now it is time to consider some of the pros and cons of a 360 recording contract "multiple rights" agreement and some clauses that are unique to these agreements.

- Record companies are entitled to a set percentage from four revenue streams of the artist in typical 360° recording contract. These revenue streams would include a portion of the artist's record sales, touring and personal appearance income, as well as publishing income and merchandise revenues.

- 270° or 180° deals "recording contract" may include only two or three revenue streams of the artist's income. These revenue streams would include a portion of the musician's record sales and publishing (180°) income or a percentage from the artist's record sales, publishing, and touring incomes (270°).

Some agreements also include "catch-all" clauses, in which the label shares in the artist's "collateral" or "ancillary" entertainment income. What this essentially means is that the record label has the right to a percentage of income generated from anything related to the musician's entertainment career that is not covered in any of the aforementioned categories, ie, touring, publishing, record sales, merchandise, appearance fees, live performances, video games, etc. In this agreement, the record label is entitled to their traditional stream of revenue from recorded music and some percentages of all revenues from the artist's entertainment career. In summary, the label shares in any way the artist makes money.

Typically, with these contracts, the artist enters into different contracts with separate contractual "advancements" encompassing the entire 360° deal. All these contracts are usually cross-collateralized with each other. This implies that all revenue generated from the various income streams can be used to pay back any advance from the label to the artist as opposed to the label using the publishing revenues solely to recoup the publishing agreement advance. Although it is hard to sell to most labels, artists are advised to try to negotiate that the different revenue streams are not cross-collateralized. The record labels are usually hesitant to accept such accommodation because they want sufficient avenues through which they can recoup their full investment.

Another important negotiation for the artist to consider or should have in their minds is whether the record label has an "active" or "passive" interest in the streams of income the record label are collecting from the artist. A passive interest is one in which the record label only earns its set percentage under the contract without having any control over or not assisting the artist to earn the revenue stream involved. In this agreement, the artist is free to enter into any deal they desire, such as a touring or publishing agreement, as long as the record label receives their percentage of the compensation.

On the other hand, an active interest exists where the record label has rights over the artist's work, which entitles them to insist that the artist signs a deal with their publishing, merchandise, or touring company. In such a situation, the artist should attempt to negotiate a smaller percentage for that particular revenue stream of income that the record label recoups the money from or is "active" in. For instance, if the artist is obligated to sign with the record label's touring company, the artist should try to reduce the percentage that the record label receives under the "360 deal" from merchandising and publishing revenues as the record label would essentially be getting paid twice; as a tour company for the artist and through the record label's 360 deal.

Even though there are many benefits as well as drawbacks to the 360 recording contracts, many record labels have come to accept them because they provide some security for the record label's finances, with the record label's knowing that there have been a lot more unsuccessful artists than commercially successful artists throughout the recording industry history. Record labels like EMI and Live Nation are some entities that show that the new additions to 360 recording contracts increase the record label's capacity to earn more profits from the artist's non-recording revenue streams of income. In many ways, since the record label's takes all of the financial risks in the beginning of the artists' career with a small chance of even recouping their investment from fronting the artist's advancements fee to the artist's tour support. If the artist's album fails to be a commercial success, the record label will not only lose on their initial investment but not gain any type of profits. So, the record label's feels by tapping into the artist's over income streams is a safer way for the record label to ensure they get a return on their investment.

Pros and Cons of Profit Split Record Deals or Net Profit Deals

If the artist has a full project "album or EP" that has not yet been released, the artist can approach a record label with a Net Profit deal whereby the record label would invest in the marketing and promotion of the artist unreleased album.

Net Profit Deals have become more popular in the past 10 to 15 years. These type of record deals were quite common with indie record labels before major record labels starting occasionally signing such contracts with artists as an alternative to the traditional type of record deal.

The idea behind this type of record deal "Profit Split Deal" is that after all expenses connected with the artist's album are recouped by the record label from the artist's record sales, any remaining profits from this point onward will be split between the artist and the record label, with the artist receiving 40-50% of those net profits.

The Basics of Net Profit Deals

Record labels usually deduct all costs related to recording the album and manufacturing of the album. The record label is also going to deduct any cost that is associated with the album's promotion, marketing, touring support, and any cash advancements made directly to the artist. All these costs has to be recouped by the record label before they can arrive at the net profits in a Net Profit Deal. After the record label makes deductions of all of these expenses and recoups recording costs from the artist's income, the label will then pay the artist the percentage of the profits stipulated in their contract (usually 50%).

Although the percentage received by an artist in a Net Profit Deal is clearly larger than the 13-17% royalty range received by artists in traditional recording contracts or royalty-based recording contracts, the artist will only receive 50% of what's left of the income from records sold after all expenses are paid.

Pros for Labels

The main advantage is that record labels do not have to make any payment to the artist until all costs that were advanced by the record label have been recouped. In today's world of music, it appeals greatly to the record label's particularly when the record label are covering most of the front-end costs.

Cons for Labels

The biggest shortcoming of these type of recording contracts for the record labels usually arises on the back end of the deal. If the revenue from records sales are more substantial than the amount the record label recoups from recording costs. In this instance, a traditional recording contract would have been more profitable for the label record than a Profit Split deal.

Pros for Artists

The reasons Net Profit deals appeal to artists are quite different from that of the record labels.

If record sales are substantial and recording costs are quite reasonable in comparison to the revenue from the album sales, the artist stands to benefit more from the profit splitting deal than with the traditional record deal.

Many artists prefer a 50-50 split of net profits as it seems fairer and a better deal in comparison to the complexities inherent in a traditional record deal. Artists typically prefer a profit split record deal, which looks more like a partnership and a collaborative relationship between the record label and the artist.

Cons for Artists

A drawback that somewhat dampens the appeal of a 50-50 partnership between the record label and the artist is the fact that even if the contract clearly affirms that net profits will be split on a 50-50 basis, in many instances, the record label actually receives more than its stipulated 50% of the net profits. Some record labels deduct an "Overhead Fee" off the top, as well as all other costs (such as recording, distribution, and promotion costs). The profit is whatever is left after these deductions are made and then the rest of the revenue is divided 50-50. If the record label ends up receiving an Overhead Fee and their share from the 50-50 split of whatever the "Net Income" will be. The record label actually ends up with a larger portion of the net profits than the artist.

> **NET PROFIT DEALS:** Below is a sample breakdown of calculations showing how the "Overhead Fee" results in the label receiving more than 50% of the net profits.

ARTIST ROYALTIES (based on a wholesale price of $10 per record received by the label from its distributor):

20,000 records sold @ $10 per record = $200,000 GROSS INCOME received by the label from its distributor.

$200,000 minus $20,000 recording costs (this is reimbursement to the Label for those costs) = $180,000

$180,000 minus $20,000 in duplication and printing costs (calculated at $1/per record) for 20,000 records = $160,000

$160,000 minus $20,000 (i.e. 100% of the $20,000 in costs incurred by the label to advertise, market, promote the record (This is reimbursement to the Label for those costs.) = $140,000 SUB-TOTAL

$140,000 minus a $30,000 "Overhead Fee" deducted and pocketed by label (based on 15% of the $300,000) = $110,000 SUB-TOTAL

½ of this amount is payable to the Artist = $55,000

½ to the Label = $55, 000 (IN ADDITION TO the $30,000 "Overhead Fee" deducted and pocketed by the Label), for a total of $85,000 to the Label

The amounts we have mentioned above are just examples of some of the seemingly unnoticed financial issues beneath Net Profit Deals. As a result of this, it is difficult to tell in advance whether a Net Profit Deal will be more or less beneficial than a standard record deal.

Some of the other disadvantages of a Net Profit Deals that an artist may face include the following:

1. **Mechanical Royalty Issues:** Artists who write songs for their own records and are signed to a standard record deal are entitled to receive mechanical royalties on all record sales periodically. These payments are made by the label in addition to the 18-20% artist royalties from their album sales and music streaming revenue. These mechanical royalties are a vital source of income for the artist.

Mechanical royalties are handled quite differently in the case of Net Profit Deals in one of two ways:

i. The mechanical royalties are either paid similarly to how they are paid in a standard record deal. In the case of Net Profit deals, the number of mechanical royalties paid to the artist will be treated as an advancement to the artist and later deducted from the artist's share if there are any net profits; or

ii. Instead of the artist receiving mechanical royalties for their original material, they will only be paid a share of net profits. The contract usually has a section that reads thus; "All monies payable to Artist hereunder shall be inclusive of any mechanical royalties which would otherwise be payable to Artist."

In the second instance, the artist does not receive revenue from mechanical royalties that would be paid in the case of a standard recording contract.

These problems are compounded by the fact that the record label usually spends money faster than it receives. So, when there is eventually a profit from the record sales, it will take a long period of time before the artist receives a share of the net profits. In the worst-case scenario - is when where the record label receives no net profits from the album sales, the artist will receive nothing from the deal. This is a case of "no artist royalties, and no mechanical royalties."

2. **Audit Issues:** This is another disadvantage of Net Profit Deals that makes it difficult and strenuous for artists to do a royalty audit with Net Profit Deals compared to standard record deals under similar circumstances. This happens because, in the case of Net Profit Deals, the artist can only know whether they have been paid the proper amount by verifying all the income and all the expenses that the label incurred on their behalf. In standard record deals, all the artist needs to do is to verify only the income received and certain types of expenses, which are recording costs, marketing, and promotion costs. Don't forget that these audits are expensive which can easily cost about $15,000 to $20,000 which are charged to the artist. These amounts are higher, particularly in the case of major record label artists who sell a large amount of records

Artists should ensure that their Net Profit Deal contract gives them strong audit rights and provides that if the label's accounting statements are off by a certain percentage, the label will then be obligated to reimburse the artist for all audit costs incurred.

3. **Merchandising:** The record label is often entitled to create and sell different forms of merchandising for each released record during the duration of the contract. For example, in Net Profit Deals, the label will have the right to manufacture and sell a new T-shirt for each record released during the term of the deal. These T-shirts will then be marketed and sold from the label's website or other usual channels. The artist then shares in the net profits from those sales.

4. This usually happens regardless of how the label record goes about the sale of such T-shirts. Since merchandising sales play a big role in the survival of artists on tour, artists entering into Net Profit Deals should either attempt to avoid giving the record label the right to sell such T-shirts and other merchan-

dise or at the very least, negotiate the best possible contractual rights and protections that give them an advantage in the long-term.

5. **Overhead Fees:** These are also referred to as Administration Fees and Marketing Fees. Most artists see these "Overhead Fees" as outrageous and questionable because the record label already received 50% of any net profits. When the deal is negotiated, these fees can either be expunged completely from the agreement or the percentage remarkably reduced.

Anti-360 Deals

A 360 deal or multiple rights deals, as we now know, is not a new industry concept. We are also familiar with how for many decades, these deals have taken advantage of a large number of artists. In today's marketplace, contracts have been created which are essentially "Anti-360 Deals." Artists no longer have to sign a 360 if they don't want to; these Anti-360 Deals enable artists to exercise more artistic control and musical leverage without losing the funding they deserve.

Artist Deals or Development Deals

This deal is based on the 360 concepts but is an agreement made between artists so the up-and-coming acts will benefit from the success of their more established and popular colleagues.

Unsigned artists can help with their recording careers by signing a development deal with a music publisher. A common approach that is used is for the publisher to guarantee the financing of a set number of high-quality studio recordings (and sometimes even a video) so that the record label will be able to hear the artist at his or her best and, if a recording artist agreement is secured, the publisher will receive royalty points on albums and singles released under the deal. For instance, the publisher might guarantee $20,000 to $30,000 to record master quality demos and if a recording artist agreement is secured, the publisher might receive a production or executive producer royalty of 1% to 3% for its efforts.

On other occasions, publishers might choose to finance an entire album of the artist's and try to sell or license the album to either an independent or major record label. Although this approach is more expensive, its value is that the publisher provides the record company with a finished product ready to be released.

An alternative to this approach is to make available an equipment fund that provides a financial cushion for the purchase of new musical equipment for the writer-performer. This can be done based on an extra advance to the writer who will have to decide what they need (maybe an extra advance of $6,000 to $15,000 to the songwriter within a specific period like 30 days after the signing of the agreement, which shall be used for the purchase of musical equipment). This fund will be spent with the mutual approval of the publisher and the songwriter (for example, "an advance of $6,000. which shall be payable by the publisher for the purchase of equipment mutually agreed to by both the artist and the publisher") or a fund which can be accessed by the writer providing invoices from the retailers which show the amount of each item purchased with the publisher paying the retailer directly.

Licensing Deal

Licensing record deals generally apply to already established artists with a large and impressive portfolio and a track record of successful album sales. This prevents the record label from having copyright or control over previous releases, particularly if an artist has released a lot of music and is offered a 360 deal.

Many indie record labels usually face the challenge of choosing between licensing and distribution deals, especially when they need their albums on the international scene. Each deal has its own benefits and drawbacks, which can have a significant impact on the artist's career.

What Is Licensing?

Licensing is the process whereby another business, a record label or a distributor, purchases the rights to an album from its original owner. They usually pay a fixed fee and then begin to act as the label for that album in the region for which they licensed the album. For instance, let's say your label is based in the US, and you have an album that you want to release in

Portugal. A Portugal-based record label will license the album from you. They now own the rights to your album and can sell it on their record label in Portugal.

The Portugal record label is responsible for producing the album, promoting it, and distributing it in their country. The monetary rewards from selling it are theirs; the only money you make is your original licensing fee. Perhaps they lose money on the album; the loss is also theirs. Your licensing fee remains with you regardless of the album's performance and sales.

What Is Distribution?

Distribution refers to the process of getting your albums into shops. When an artist signs a distribution record deal, the artist will only make money on the records that they sell while the record label is responsible for manufacturing and promotion of the album. If the artist generates a ton of revenue from sales, the artist gets to keep it all. But if the artist loses money on the album, it is their lost, not the record labels. Licensing and distribution also have benefits and drawbacks. Record Label's record need to be in the driver's seat to build a name and control their releases and artists. There have been several cases where an independent record label signs an artist that begins to generate a lot of buzz, with major record labels approaching them, wanting to license or distribute the artist album for them. In this case, a licensing recording deal would be ideal for this type of situation since the major record label has more resources and covers bigger market territories than independent record labels. Since the major record label has the resources required to give the artist better promotion and marketing, and the cash from the licensing deal could be just what the independent record label needs to properly push the album. Generally, it's better to go for the artist or the independent record label to sign a distribution deal with the major record label rather than licensing deal because they would still receive the royalties and licensing and sync for the album.

However, licensing deals offers independent recording labels more benefits when it comes to getting albums on the international market in the following ways:

- Local record labels based in certain international territories know those markets better; have existing relationships with the media, retailers, and distributors; therefore, they will have better tools at their disposal to promote the artist and their album.

- Distributing records overseas can be expensive; local record labels may need the services of a PR company or radio plugger in those countries to help generate some press and publicity for the artists and the album before any retail stores begin to stock albums, which can get extremely costly.

- Licensing deals improve cash flow for the independent record labels or the artist; and generates revenue upfront.

- Licensing deals place the burden of risks on the major record label obtaining the album's licensing rights since they are up-fronting all the costs.

The most remote risk associated with licensing deals comes up if the album is a big hit in the new territory, making the licensing fee paid to the independent record label pale in comparison. It's a gamble that is worth the risk for small independent record labels because managing an overseas portfolio is both time-consuming, requires a lot of effort and is costly.

Distribution Deal

The record label pays all bills that have to do with press and distribution; other bills are the responsibility of the artist or smaller independent record label. Distribution record deals are commonly used when the artist has generated a lot of buzz that the major record label wants to take advantage of.

EP Deals

Artist's and the record labels collaborate to produce an EP, "Extended Play." The record label provides the best strategy for marketing; however, their collaborative relationship will not be announced to the public. This allows the record label to test the waters before signing the artist on a full-time basis.

EP stands for "extended play record" or "extended play" in the music industry. An EP comprises songs often created for promotional use. It also covers single and full-length albums. EPs are usually four to six songs in length and are generally produced from an artist's unreleased original tracks.

The most common reason artists release EPs is to use them as promotional tools to grow a fan base. EPs are often used to introduce a new artist, sustain public interest in an artist until the release of their full-length album, or help promote a tour. EPs are also used by artists as giveaways and incentives for joining mailing lists or to help sell concert tickets.

There are more reasons artists create EPs; these include:

- Providing solutions for artists who want to release something more solid than a single track but can't afford the studio time they need to record a full-length album—which usually contains about 10 to 12 songs.

- EP's are also used by some artists to experiment with a new style of music or because they want to try out in less commercial sounds than their full-length albums feature.

- EPs are also sometimes used to release the B-side of a hit song, as well as unreleased songs that were cut when the full-length album was recorded in the studio.

Major Label Deals

Major record labels pay for everything under this type of recording contract. Their artists also get a large advance which the record label is expected to recoup from the artist. The royalty rate for major label recording contracts deals are pretty low, and the record label retains rights to the music of the artist even after they part ways.

Single Deals

This recording contract is based purely on single tracks instead of full albums, and it has become very common in Europe. It really consists of a contractual agreement where the record label invests some money in order to produce the single and promote it. This allows the record label not to sign the artist for a long term unless the artist single performs well on the charts and sales well. In this recording contract, the record label usually does not spend a lot of money on the marketing and promotion of the single. Black Moon in the '90s started with a single. As the artist putting out one song, you may not get the funding you desire. The single's recording contract says something like this "If this song sells, the record label will sign you for this period for this amount of money."

Why a single deal?

As the artist with high prospects for success, the following are some of the reasons you should consider a single deal recording contract:

1. Even though you will give up the rights to one of your songs, the rest of your songs still belong to you.

2. With adequate support from the record label; the song is successfully released and begins to be aired regularly; people will want to hear more projects from you. The success of this song's take-off could even make them purchase your other songs. You know you own these songs 100%.

3. Successful promotion of the song could lead to an increase in merchandise sales, ticket sales, and better

touring opportunities. Like you know already, these additional income streams are yours 100%.

4. The record label that takes responsibility for promoting and publishing your single track will not make a substantial financial commitment because it's just one high-quality song. Their aim is to leverage the relationships they already have with radio and publishing companies to make money off the one song. The record label's approach these deals with caution but also know that it is potentially profitable for them and can draw in bigger opportunities for signed artists without going up to a 5/6 album deal contract.

Ownership of Masters and Publishing

When a song is recorded, there is the idea and the actual tangible recording. For example, a CD is a tangible product; the idea is the publishing. In a publishing deal of $200, 000, an artist is signing away their intellectual property. If anyone tries to use this, they have to pay a publishing fee.

The masters recording is the actual copy of the project, like the CD of an album. It is typically referred to as the official recording of a performance in a tangible medium like a CD, cassette, or an mp3 from which copies can be made. Recordings that are bought or downloaded are not considered masters; these are copies of the original masters.

Most indie artists are of the impression that they should own their masters because it is their intellectual property and they contributed the performance and often pay for the recording. In other cases, the owners can be involved because copyright and master's ownership usually varies based on certain requirements of the law and contract.

When the artist signs a record deal or a recording deal, they sign away their recording, meaning that the label owns the recording of that music. A recording agreement states that the record label will own all master recordings done by the artist during the term of the contract.

On the publishing side, if the artist writes a record and signs away their publishing in a publishing deal, the label now owns the composition of work. This means that whoever plays a song publicly, let's say on the piano written by an artist, the label must be paid a publishing fee, the same applies to when a line from the song is done by some other person.

Artists who intend to fully own their masters must have well-documented agreements in place with all parties involved in the recording process: the studio, engineers, producers, and hired musicians. These agreements should state in clear terms that the artist owns the masters and include language whereby these contributors to the recording will transfer the rights to their contribution in the masters to the artist.

Since these contracts are complex with many components and legal wording, they should be drafted by an experienced music attorney. Artists who are unable to hire an attorney for this purpose can utilize DIY templates that are available online.

Merchandising

Tour merchandise like concert T-shirts, face caps and stickers, or simply "merchandising," is a significant source of income for many artists and bands. Merchandising deals are complex involving large music merchandising companies and are beyond the capacity of a friend who can make or sell t-shirts at the back of their van.

These merchandising companies license the names of artists, image, produce and sell other items, paying the artist royalties. Although merchandising deals are similar to record label deals, they have some important differences.

Points to Note in Merchandise Deals

The royalty an artist will be paid by the merchandise company for featuring their name, artwork, logo, and album name is clearly an important point in any merchandising deal. Tour merchandising royalties can be calculated in two ways: percentage deals and profit splits.

1. Percentage Deals

Here, the artist will be paid a fixed percentage of gross sales of their goods. Gross sales typically mean sales minus all taxes and credit card fees paid by the merchandising manufacturers. If the artist receives a percentage of their royalties, a provision can be worked into the contract, which states that the royalty rate will increases as certain sales thresholds are attained.

2. Profit Splits

Profit splits are based on net sales (not gross sales). In this approach, the merchandising company deducts all of its expenses from the sales income and then shares what is left with the artist at a fixed rate. Profit splits are a norm in foreign royalty deals and deals for stadium shows and festivals.

Concert bills or programs are also often sold on a split, even if the rest of the tour merchandising is sold under a percentage deal.

Keep in mind that if an artist chooses to have their merchandise company outsource the manufacture or design of any merchandise, their royalty rate will be reduced on these items than other merchandise. This is because the merchandising company will end up bearing the cost of the outside designer, and the lower royalty rate serves as its way of recouping the costs.

Tour Merchandise Advances

Like record deals, the artists also get an advancement on a tour merchandising deal. These advancements are usually recoupable by the merchandising company, which implies that the artist is obligated to pay back the advancement.

The failure of the artist to tour with the time frame specified in the contract is one reason out of many that can put them in the unfortunate position of repaying their merchandising advancement. Refusing to play to audiences the sizes expected when the deal was signed is another reason artists end up repaying merchandise advancements. In a situation where the artist decides to terminate the tour deal, they will have to pay back the advancement with interest.

Advancements paid to artists typically vary in size depending on the artist's bargaining power, the term of the tour, and the size of the artist's fan base and venues for the tour.

Tour contracts should clearly state the amount and terms of the advancements.

Terms

The term refers to the length of the contract. For tour merchandising, the artists are usually signed for one album cycle or until the advancements has been repaid, depending on which term is longer. Artists who repay their advancement but fail to release another album are

typically under contract with a tour merchandising company forever, except they renegotiate the contract with the help of an experienced attorney.

Chapter 4
RECOUPABLE COSTS

Recoupable Cost "Major vs. Indie"

What most people consider a success for most major label artists is a façade. It's basically smoke and mirrors. This illusion is backed by the substantial amounts these billion-dollar labels invest in signing their and executing it in a way that appears natural and widespread.

I will give a monetary breakdown of campaigns involving Indies and major record labels highlighting and explaining the major differences between these two types of labels for folks who may not understand how things truly work in the industry.

The major difference between an artist signed to a major record label and an independent record label is that Indies retain a sizeable share of the income from their project. A major artist will be lucky to receive even a dollar from record sales after repaying the record label back their recoupable expenses. In some record deals in which an indie artist partners with an investor to sponsor the project's promotion, they tend to keep about 50% of every dollar generated from sales.

We now consider some examples to illustrate record sales of Indies vs. the money made by artists signed to a major record label. Although these examples may not be all-inclusive, they are true-to-life.

Major Label Artist Example

Major record label artists goes Double-Platinum selling 2,000,000 iTunes album downloads at $23.99. iTune takes out 30%, leaving a gross of $16.793 for each download sold. We will keep things simple by saying that all the sales were via iTunes. Therefore 2,000,000 copies x $16.973 = $33,586,500

The artist deal is 10% of record sales; 10% of $33.5 million is $3,359,000.

In reality, the artist will not receive a check for this amount of money. The artist has to first repay all recoupable costs that the record label invested in the making, marketing and promotion of the artist album. The artists also have to repay the advancement that they received before recording the album. (remember recoupable expenses?)

Total recoupable expenses (advertising, promotion, video shot, artwork, recording, and promotion, radio, etc.) = $1,545,000

Artist owes the label $1,545,000 after selling $20,000,000 worth of music.

Remember that this debt doesn't include the advance that the artist got when signing to the major record label. This amount is also recoupable and must be repaid.

Indie: Indie Artist Example

An Indie artist sponsored by an investor sells 2,000,000 downloads at $23.99. Keep in mind that iTunes takes 30% of that off the top, leaving a gross of $16.793 for each download. Once again, we will keep things simple by saying that all the sales were via iTunes. So 2,000,000 copies x $16.973 = $33,946,000. The artist has a 50/50 split on sales with the record label; 50% of $33,946,000 = $16,973,000.

In the case of the major record label, the artist repays the company all the money that was invested into the project. Let's assume the indie artist has to cover expenses that amount to $1,545,000; they will still earn over $15 million after repaying all costs back to the indie record label.

In summary, an indie artist who sells 1/10th of the amount of a major label artist is in still better positioned to make a larger profit margin in music sales. In the interim, if the artist sells a lot less records than the indie artists, they may not become as famous and internationally known as the major label artist. The indie artist may not grace red carpet events like the Grammy's, AMA's, VMA's, BET awards, etc., since the indie artist may not be known by the masses or the music executives who are putting together these events. The indie artist may not immediately become a music phenomenon? But eventually, these indie artists can reach these landmarks with a lot of hard work and consistency.

In the music business, the allure and popularity of major record label artists have blinded many upcoming artists and made them walk dead ends where they have fame but not fortune.

An indie artist with the right focus, drive, and determination can make millions from their craft via numerous income channels and platforms that include but are not limited to merchandising online, website hits, YouTube, and Twitter views without the "well-oiled" major record label machine.

I'm not saying working with a major record label is a bad move. If artists work their careers correctly and gain sufficient leverage and popularity, the artist can actually get a great deal from major record labels.

Tour support "Major vs. Indie"

Tour support is financial support provided to the touring artist to cover any expenses incurred on a tour. These tour expenses could include traveling, crew accommodations, equipment cost and rental, vehicle rental or other transportation costs, and the list continues. Tours can be expensive and can often end up cost record labels more money than they original spent signing the new artist. Although tours are expensive and very risky investment for the record label and the tour promoters. But ultimately, the pros of touring outweigh the risk involved, so that is why record labels and tour promoters still chose to invest in tour support. It is necessary for an artist to tour in order to promote their album and to open up another revenue stream. Touring also allows for the artist to become known in different markets that they are performing in during the tour gaining new fans and increasing their album sales at the same time. Another way that artists are able to receive tour support is from random companies who will upfront the artist a certain amount of cash in order to be an endorser on the tour.

Tours often end up costing more than they earn for newer artists since touring is necessary to promote the artist record's and gain exposure in new markets. The record label may decide to upfront funds to the artist to keep them on the road touring. In the past, tours were funded by the record label. Today, tour support are mainly financed by larger live promotion company's "Live Nation and Ticket Master" other tour support comes from large business conglomerates, drink, and sports companies with no direct involvement in the music. Recording contracts generally provide that tour support money is recoupable against an artist's royalties. So, ultimately the artist will have to repay either a portion of the tour support or the entire amount of the tour support the artist received if the artist did not negotiate for the record label to cover a portion of the tour support that the artist received from the record label.

Indie/Small Record Labels Tour Support

Touring is an expensive promotional exercise used to market the artist and their music. This is one reason tour support is hard to come by for many artists especially indie artists. It is a common trend for only the biggest music artists to receive a substantial amount of tour support from their record label. Listed below are some reasons for this:

- With the shrinking of physical album sales as a result of digital releases, Indie labels may no longer be able to foot the bill if album sales revenue continue to decrease.

- The returns on tour support are uncertain, especially promotional tours that are aimed at raising the profile of the artist to build a fan base. Tours are designed to help the artist to become more appealing and to find a core audience. This does not necessarily translate into increased album sales and music streaming revenue to offset the record label's tour support investment.

Even before the digitization of music, small record label's support for touring artists suffered from these and other internal challenges that major record labels do not face. Tours often succeeded in expanding the fan base of the artist and facilitated the artist's move from the independent record label to a major record label.

There have been several different scenarios in the music industry where artists were supported by an independent record label and moved on to a major record label without paying off their debt back to their independent record label. Unfortunately, this is a trend that has come to stay and has become a norm in the music industry.

This may be the underlying reason there is little or no tour support at all for most artists who are signed to an independent record label. The current attitude by tour management and record labels now tends to be along the lines that either a new artist will succeed somehow without tour support. Major Record Label Tour Support

Tour support paid by the record label is recoupable "most cases", so it's advisable to agree on a limit on a reasonable budget for obvious reasons.

Artists who go on tour to promote a record release should not forget that the financial commitment "tour support" made by the record label will be recouped out their album sales and music streaming royalties, so it is highly recommended to spend the tour support advancement responsibly.

By nature of the music industry, new artists often need to be heavily supported by their record labels to start off their careers. The amount of tour support needed is largely dependent on the current fanbase of the artist. Pop artists typically require more financial support than Rock acts. The inclusion of a backing band, an orchestra, or extra props can raise tour costs. Tour support typically costs major record companies upwards of $100,000 per tour.

Example of Indie Tour Cost

In 2014, Pomplamoose (Jack Conte and Nataly Dawn) had a 28-day tour of the US. They detailed what it took to organize the tour. Throughout the tour, they played 24 shows in 23 cities and sold a little under $100,000 in tickets. 1129 tickets were sold in San Francisco.

This was the response of Conte to the particular question "what does it feel like to have "made it" as a band?" their fans repeatedly ask them; "Though it's a fair question to ask of a band with a hundred million views on YouTube, the thought of Pomplamoose having "made it" is, to me, ridiculous."

He pointed out that he considers Nataly and himself fortunate to be making music for a living. "Having the opportunity to play music as a career is a dream come true. But the phrase "made it" does not properly describe Pomplamoose. Pomplamoose is "making it." And every day, we bust our asses to continue "making it," but we most certainly have not "made it," according to Conte.

Here is a breakdown of how their Fall Tour went in Conte's words:

"In order to plan and execute our Fall tour, we had to prepare for months, slowly gathering risk and debt before selling a single ticket. We had to rent lights. And book hotel rooms. And rent a van. And assemble a crew. And buy road cases for our instruments. And rent a trailer. And…all of that required an upfront investment from Nataly and me. We don't have a label lending us "tour support." We put those expenses right on our credit cards; $17,000 on one credit card and $7,000 on the other, to be more specific. And then we planned (or hoped) to make that back in ticket sales. We also knew that once we hit the road, we would be paying our band and crew on a weekly basis. One week of salaries for four musicians and two crew members (front of house engineer and tour manager) cost us $8794. That came out to $43,974 for the tour.

We built the tour budget ourselves and modeled projected revenue against expenses. Neither of us had experience with financial modeling, so we just did the best we could. With six figures of projected expenses, "the best we could" wasn't super comforting. The tour ended up costing us $147,802 to produce and execute."

The Figures

- **Expenses**

    $26,450 (Production expenses: equipment rental, lights, lighting board, van rental, trailer rental, road cases, backline.)

    $17,589 (Hotels and food for 28 nights for the tour, plus a week of rehearsals)

    $11,816 (Gas, airfare, parking tolls)

    $5,445 (Insurance)

    $48,094 (Salaries and per diems)

    $21,945 (Manufacturing merchandise, publicity, supplies, shipping)

    $16,463 (Commissions)

Good enough, Pomplamoose made some money to offset some of these expenses. Here is a summary of the income from the tour:

- **Income**

    $97,519 (Their cut of ticket sales) Almost 72% of the tour income came from the tickets fans bought.

    $29,714 (Merch sales, Hats, t-shirts, CDs, posters 22% of their tour income)

    $8,750 (Sponsorship from Lenovo)

    Lenovo gave them three laptops and some cash. (Remember what we said about the invaluable role of investors/tour support in an Indie band?) Tour sponsor serves to provide financial aid and light at the end of a dark tunnel preventing certain bankruptcy.

In summary

Pomplamoose made $135,983 in total income for their tour and had $147,802 in expenses, with a loss of $11,819.

In Conte's words, "This isn't a sob story. We knew it would be an expensive endeavor, and we still chose to make the investment. We could have played a duo show instead of hiring six people to tour with us. That would have saved us over $50,000, but it was important at this stage in Pomplamoose's career to put on a wild and crazy rock show. We wanted to be invited back to every venue, and we wanted our fans to bring their friends next time. The loss was an investment in future tours."

Importance of Social Media when being an Indie Artist

In today's music world and business, it's no longer enough to just make music and release it. While it's not unusual to just release music, go viral and kick start your music career, it's also not out of place to leverage available online resources and platforms.

The somewhat skewed playing field for music producers and artists in the past has now been leveled, making social media a good option for artists.

What does Social Media offer?

- Social media provides artists free and ample opportunity to market themselves and become visible to a global audience. Any artist who wants to make music as a career and earn a living from it should look to take advantage of every opportunity to advance their career. Social media provides free opportunities that few platforms can offer.

- Social media provides a platform to engage with your fans. The artist to know who their target audience is and how to grab their attention. Without the artist knowing this, it will be tough to build a successful career. With social media, artists can now get more of their fans to listen to their music and build relationships with them.

- Social media provides a large target audience. There are several different social media networks like Instagram, Twitter, Facebook, YouTube, and Tik Tok that provides a large community of prospective fans for artists to show off their projects through images, audio, and videos. In the blink of an eye, you can share your latest release with someone in Jamaica, chat with someone in Sweden about your latest show, live stream your studio session to thousands, and sell tickets for your next show through their own website or blog.

Ways you can Use Social Media

There are many ways you can leverage social media as an artist. We will now look at some of the ways you can utilize social media, and I will recommend that you put all of them to good use.

1. Build a Community

A key component of the online world that has made many businesses and individuals successful is "traffic." Traffic refers to people who check out your projects, make a purchase or a referral. One of the fantastic things about the internet and social media is the power of online communities. These groups of people meeting on the Internet virtually can make it possible for artists to easily get into the masses eyes and achieve success within the music industry without much difficulty. With a community, you can easily get your message or music across to a wider audience and keep the conversation going on your social media platforms. More importantly, building a community helps you connect with your target audience and enhance your music career.

Here are some ways you can build a community on social media:

- Connect with people individually: This will help build a personal connection and trust, which are necessary for building a responsive and loyal community. Send people direct messages, make posts on their wall, give them shout-outs, tag them to your posts or send them a video or voice message. Use all channels that provide a direct line of communication to your audience. It always works.

- Live stream: When you live stream, your fans and prospects get to know who you are as a person. It also gives your audience a platform to interact with you in real-time. You can live stream a Q&A or studio session. You can live stream when you are getting ready for your next show or tour or anything that you know will bring you closer to your fans/audience.

2. Provide Value

Think like an entrepreneur because your career is also a business. The amount of time or money your fans will be willing to pay for an experience or product depends on the value they think they will get out of it. Providing value is a vital and often overlooked step when artists begin the journey of building a community and career on social media platforms. What exactly does providing value mean? Providing value could mean giving your audience a solution to their pain without invading their private space, something that they find beneficial, useful, or insightful. Naturally, we tend to like and express gratitude to people who offer us help without charging us. The key is not to demand or expect anything in return from your fans or audience when you are providing value. Providing value builds trust and loyalty between the artist and their fans.

Here are some ways you can provide value as an artist:

- Give away your new track for free (remember what we said about EPs)

- Help other artists publicize their music on your social media platforms

- Occasionally give away free merchandise

- Take the time to get to know your fans. Be Sincere!!!

Not everyone on social media is sincere. Many lie about who they are, what they do, and portray a fake life just to look a certain way front for everything in their life. For many social media users, their projects are mostly a façade. People appreciate and respond best to sincerity. Just be real, down-to-earth, and humane. This might initially generate some negative response from those who don't know and understand, but your community and followers will stand with you, share your message and repeatedly patronize you.

Chapter 5
REVENUE

In the past record, sales was the main driver of revenue for record labels. While artists always had to depend on other sources of income like touring, merchandising, endorsements, and other entertainment industry related incomes.

Business-minded artists should look to maximize all potential income streams. Access to sufficient revenue can help you plan adequately for the projects you can execute in the short-term and long term. Regardless of the size of your vision, you will need funding to make it come true. Your business plan basically attracts investors and sponsors and provides them with information on how their investments will be maximized.

Some of the most common revenue sources for artists include physical sales, merchandise, music publishing, sync deals, streaming, brand partnerships/endorsements and live touring/live shows. Below, we will have an in-depth account of each revenue stream; recording revenue and performance revenue.

Indie Artists Revenue

Recording Revenue

Physical Music Sales

While physical music sales have taken some hits since the turn of the century, they are still a formidable source of income for artists. If the artist album sells enough copies to repay the recoupable cost associated with the making of the album and the artist's advancement. After all the recoupable costs are repaid to the record label, "if signed to an indie record label," the artist will begin to receive their percent of the album sales royalties.

CDs, cassettes, vinyl records, tapes, etc., can be made available either through a distributor, the artist's own web store or at the merchandise table at events or concerts. Although physical music sales could be the weakest source or strongest source of revenue, they are incredibly cheap to produce, and limited vinyl records can be sold as a collector's item.

How much of a profit you make from this income source depends on the genre, the market you are in, and the strength of your sales strategy and the overall marketing and promotion of the album itself. Some artists still succeed in making reasonable revenue from sales of physical records; this may not be the case for the majority of up-and-coming and mid-career artists.

The most effective way to do this is to produce CDs and other physical records that can be sold as part of your merchandise. They can be sold individually or in a bundled with other merchandise items like face caps, stickers, and t-shirts.

Digital Downloads

Artists can sell downloads of their single tracks or the complete album via digital retailers like Amazon, iTunes, Tunecore, CDBaby and etc. Although digital sales experienced a little decline in 2013, they still account for a good amount of overall music sales throughout the world. Digital downloads remain one of the most common channel for indie artists to distribute their music though.

Streaming & Subscription-based Services

At the onset of digital streaming, many artists were quick to dismiss it as a viable source of income. Today, a handful of streaming platforms such as SoundCloud, iTunes, Spotify, Pandora, and others now serves as a major revenue source for these record labels and artists. Music streaming and subscription services have become the new force to be reckoned with for many artists who make money in the digital music world. Reports showed that revenue from streaming services grew by a staggering 51.3% in 2013, offsetting declining sales in other digital markets. Although payouts from digital streaming services are much smaller than traditional record sales, they add up over time and provide a healthy source of income revenue for artists especially since music streaming income is a residual revenue stream for the artist.

In addition to being a valuable income source, music streaming services also act as social platforms where new listeners can be introduced to your work regularly by alerts or notifications from the streaming service itself, thereby allowing you to build a dedicated fan base that can be monetized in the long term. Other lucrative income streams like touring, live shows, and merchandise.

The artist has to go through a digital retailer or distributor to get your music on all the available music streaming services. There are lots of artist-friendly services; some allow artists to upload an unlimited amount of music while retaining 100% of their rights for a one-time subscription fee "DistroKid."

Neighboring Rights

Neighboring rights refer to public performance royalties due to you as an artist (a sound recording copyrights owner). If your master recordings are publicly performed and broadcasted on channels Spotify, Sirius XM, public devices, MTV, and terrestrial radio, you are eligible to earn neighboring rights royalties. This is completely different from music publishing (royalties artists earn from public broadcasts of their music) which we will soon look at.

Let's say you performed on a sound recording that has been released to the public, you are eligible to collect royalties from a music licensing company like Re:Sound, but you must register with them or their partner organizations like ACTRA, MROC, to access these funds. Record labels can access neighboring rights royalties by registering with AVLA or SOPROQ (Quebec).

Mechanical License Fees

A mechanical license refers to the agreement by which recorded material is placed on a physical carrier, like a CD, tape, or record. It grants the licensee the right to reproduce and distribute a copyrighted composition in an audio format. The owner of the copyright for the recorded material has to grant this permission on a song-by-song basis and is entitled to receive a fee from the manufacturer of the physical medium on which the recording will be distributed. In the US,

Harry Fox Agency and Music Reports are the organizations responsible for administering these fees, while in Canada, it is the CMRRA.

These agencies collect the mechanical royalties on physical mediums, from digital downloads, streaming, webcast, radio/broadcast, etc., that are owed to the artist from the digital service providers on behalf of its clients and pays these royalties to them.

Film & TV Licensing

Although challenging to access, licensing for Film and TV is one of the most lucrative revenue streams available to artists. The film & television industry thrives off of maintaining an air of suspense, mystery, and glitz, and the practice of music licensing is also similar.

These sync deals have gained significant popularity since the decline of traditional record sales, and they enable artists to make money by having their music aired on some form of visual media (film, TV shows, video games, etc.)

It's quite difficult for an artist to access music supervisors directly, as most of them purposefully avoid contact with artists and choose to go through trusted channels such as brokers (professional song "pitchers"), labels, and music publishers. Licensing for Film & TV often consists of two distinct sources of revenue – upfront licensing and sync fees; which range from as little as $0 for an indie film to the tens of thousands for television commercials and feature films, and back-end royalties (resulting from performance rights).

You don't need to be signed to a record label or have a significant following to land a sync deal. Your music just has to be great if you hope to secure this deal. You will need instrumental versions of your recorded music and versions with clean lyrics (no swearing). The best way to submit your music for sync is to sign with a broker or music publisher that will pitch your music for you.

Music Publishing

This is significant yet easily overlooked and often misunderstood source of income. Songs and recordings are all intellectual property that comes with a set of rights. When these compositions are used or covered by artists, the owner(s) of the property is entitled to royalties.

Organizations that use this intellectual property are required to pay a license fee annually from which royalties are distributed. The process of collecting and managing royalties can be somewhat complicated; hence, most artists sign with a publishing company to do it on their behalf. These publishing companies make money through commission and also render other services to their artists, such as pitching music for sync deals.

You are entitled to royalties if you make recordings and have your works used by others. I recommend that you sign to a music publisher as soon as you begin releasing new music; this ensures that you receive all royalties you're owed when your music is performed or played publicly.

Performance Revenue

Live Shows

Live performances are a fantastic source of income for artists considering several methods that are at the disposal of artists.

1. Share of ticket sales or "guarantee": It could also be an agreed combination of both from the venue or promoter of the show.

2. Performing Rights or rights associated with the public performance of a copyrighted composition or musical work. Royalties are paid by host venues to SOCAN (or BMI/ASCAP in the US) who then, in turn, distribute them to the registered owners of the copyright of the composition, which can be a solo artist if they are self-published, or a publishing company who in turn pays the artists. Anytime a work owned by an artist is performed in public (live on stage, broadcast on the radio or television, or as background music in a hotel, store, or cafe) copyright law requires the artist to be compensated.

Merchandise

Merchandise is also a valuable source of revenue for most artists. While clothing like t-shirts is often the go-to product for merchandise, the sales of other hand goods like stickers and posters, bottle-openers, mugs, bags, face caps, hoodies, and other items of merchandise can account for a substantial portion of artist revenue.

The key is to successfully sell merchandise is to determine your target audience and what their buying habits are. Settling on the right merchandise items and coming up with a realistic plan for marketing and sales (including recouping your costs) is vital. Today, merchandise is often handled by large merchandising companies. Merchandise can be sold online at a marked-up price through intermediary vendors or your own web store, but the costs associated with shipping and customs brokering are often prohibitive. If you tour a lot with a band or background singers, having a wide range of merchandise is a key source of money when you are on the road; this strategy can allow the artists to rake in a lot of cash.

Different Revenue Streams for Artists

Advertising

If your YouTube channel is popular with a lot of subscribers or you have a website or blog with substantial traffic, you might consider joining an ad network such as YouTube's Partner program to monetize your channel or Google's AdSense program to place ads on your website.

If you make posts about products such as instruments, recording gear, books, other music, etc. on your blog, or social media accounts, you can also join Amazon's Affiliate Program and make money through referral-based sales.

Sponsorships & Endorsements

Much like sync deals, sponsorships and endorsements have seen significant traction as a major source of income for artists. This happens when an artist makes money by either endorsing a brand's product or service or working with a brand to create a signature product as many do today. We have seen this happen with musical instrument manufacturers, clothing lines, social media app developers, etc.

They can be done in different ways; the artist gets free merchandise in exchange for using and promoting a product or they also can be straight-up cash sponsorships in exchange for an endorsement. They often come with exclusivity clauses and terms, as brands aim to get as much value as they can from the deal.

Investors or Sponsors

Investors are also a good source of funding for artists. These are usually very wealthy and influential people who choose to invest in music for many reasons. Getting them to invest in your career can be difficult, but one way of getting attention is to volunteer your act at charity fundraisers or perform for free at high-end private functions.

Crowd Funding

Today, crowd-funding campaigns have become the way various artists fund their ventures and projects. It depends largely on the popularity and loyalty of your fan base. There is no guarantee that a funding campaign will always succeed, but it can be a useful tool.

It's important to research what makes a successful crowd funding campaign before launching yours. One reason many campaigns have failed is that the artist's assumed just because they are passionate about their music, every other person had the same drive.

In the past, it was a myth for DIY artists to be financially successful. Nowadays, independent artists can now make more money than they ever did. The old barriers created by major record label distribution have crumbled; things have been this way for over a decade. The Internet and social media now make promotion faster, easier and cheaper than ever before. With home recording, crowd-sourced artwork, and other cost-effective tools, Indie artists can now be financially successful; many are doing it.

Though the artist's do not make all their revenue solely from selling recorded music, record sales certainly bring in money, Indie artists are usually quite successful, generally gross $20,000 to $50,000 from sound recordings annually. These figures are for artists who have a large collection of songs and a sizeable fan base.

Indie artists who may not be as famous as their counterparts on major record labels consistently enjoy profitable careers. Indie artists who are making a profit generally fall into one or more of these groups:

- **YouTube**

YouTube is a platform that provides incredible opportunities for all types of artists including Indie artists to reach audiences globally with their music, thereby leveling the field and enabling emerging and unsigned artists to compete with mainstream artists thanks to its technology. The reality today is that many of these artists make a good living from their channels and built thriving independent music careers from YouTube.

In comparison to professional studio time at TV and radio stations of the past, costs are minimal. Distribution costs are almost zero, enabling artists a platform to build a fan base with steady releases of covers before releasing their own original content. There has been a steady rise in earnings for independent creators whose music and videos are administered on YouTube, with the casualness of the content also allowing for more rapid creation than one might find for "official" recorded projects.

With a few clicks, artists are also provided valuable data utilizing YouTube's analytics, allowing them to know who their fans are and where their fans are. This in turn, helps them create content that resonates with their audience.

Companies like Maker Studio have grown to help artists monetize their music with better-leveraged ad rates, production assistance, and channel cross-promotion. Once networks are ramped up with quality content, successful solo artists in this area can earn mid-to-high five figures in income and will not have to split it

- **Live Touring**

Though moving from one city to another is usually tough and expensive, many artists have developed new ways to make tours work. If you need a type of show that requires minimal promotion but a lot in return, you should consider house concerts. House concerts allow artists to nurture relationships with fans and make thousands per night.

Social networks have made the promotion of live tours in new cities cheaper and easier to find a large number of "super fans" that might bring friends to the show. Smart artists also tour in regions where they know a fan base already exists from a mailing list and social network data mining.

Once the shows kick-off and the audience is primed to enjoy the performance, artists can sell their merchandise. Because fans are within reach, creative merchandise items like wallets, sunglasses, jewelry, and handbags can be sold, thereby leading to increased sales. When this is added up, artists who make an effort to utilize these approaches can raise mid-to-high five figures in profit. Even though touring can be challenging, artists who choose to leverage this income source will earn more.

Major Record Label Artists Revenue

Like I have pointed out in previous sections of this guide, all records have two sides, with each one having distinct income streams. In the business of music publishing, revenue is derived from writing release standard songs and finding ways to leverage the work of songwriters. In the business of recorded music, on the other hand, revenue comes from recording songs and leveraging the resulting sound recordings for profit.

On the master side, record companies and artists exploit four revenue streams: sales, streaming, master use license fees, and royalties from digital audio transmissions. Recorded music sales for a long time have been the way fans have connected with artists. Today, this connection has changed and keeps changing as business goals transition from purchasing toward streaming.

While earnings from these four revenue streams may come majorly from purchases made by fans, master use licensing in film, radio, TV, advertising or video games implies finding new channels for music to be used by companies and brands. Lastly, the digital performance of masters (like music publishing's public performance royalties) represents a revenue source coming from non-interactive streaming.

Recorded Music Sales

Figure Out Which Record Label

The music business did not begin with records. It began with sheet music deals — one of the four significant music publishing income streams. It once represented the entire music business; however, after World War I, records started to surpass sheet music in prominence.

The rise of jazz was a huge factor: at that point. Jazz could be heard only in specific clubs in some cities like New York, Chicago, and New Orleans. However, word spread quickly, and music lovers, hungry for the music, looked to records which were on shellac plates played at 78 rpm on gadgets known as gramophones to hear these new sounds. The appeal and demand of this product made huge waves that allowed for the viral spread of many record labels that recorded and produced music in a wide range of genres.

In the 20th Century, records were the dominant channel through which consumers connected with music. Despite the constant change in formats (from 78 to vinyl, at that point to tape, to CD, and afterward to downloads), consumers constantly listened to records, and record labels joyfully kept on driving and leveraging record deals, splitting the royalties they received with their artists.

Streaming Music

Two occasions at the start of the 21st Century changed the landscape of the recorded music business. Firstly, the creation and introduction of the mp3 caused unrest for most major record labels because the immense distribution networks they had developed for tangible records could not handle the spread of digital music. Secondly, unable to deal with this change and challenge alone, major record labels had to play the waiting game for streaming services to transform how music was consumed by fans.

This change made doing business a huge challenge, especially as piracy, file-sharing, and overpriced items all negatively affected their income and at the same time, altered customer behavior and preferences.

We are currently in the period of the transition to music streaming. Music Streaming (regardless of whether interactive or non-interactive) represents over 62% of all music consumption. Therefore, the record labels that persevered and surmounted the extensive misfortunes of the later parts of the 2010s are gaining substantial profits in the mid-2020s.

Unlike when record labels sold records and artists received a percent of the sales from every sale, payouts from streaming music are more complicated. Music Streaming income received by Digital Service Providers (DSPs) is a combination of monthly subscriptions and advertising, and an algorithm determines how much a record label will receive. This percentage is divided by track, after which the record company pays out to the artist based on their record deal.

Music streaming services are here to stay. Generally speaking, with income streams consistently expanding, it is not yet clear whether the current payment strategy will keep on determining how DSPs, record labels, and artists split the money. Whatever happens, it remains obvious that accessibility and the ease of digital distribution have leveled the marketplace and welcomed more independent artists to deliver their records close by those of high-profile superstars.

Master Use Licensing

Regardless of whether consumers continue to stream or keep buying their music, a marketplace still exists for artists outside regular fans. Consider how much music you hear in one day and how little of it you really picked. Music is everywhere; we hear it while we are on the go, in restaurants, train stations, bars and clubs, offices, and public spaces, we are not even talking about film and TV, video games, and advertising. Corporations often love to connect their brands and products to artists who are popular at the time. Finding viable and appealing licensing opportunities helps them make this connection. The decision to make use of an artist's work by an organization requires a license, and each placement presents an opportunity for the record label and the recording artist to explore their copyright and make some money from the use of their sound recordings.

Digital Audio Transmissions

Interactive music is music that allows consumers to make selections and choose their music on-demand like streaming. Non-interactive music on the other hand, is represented by digital and satellite radio, internet transmissions, and webcasting. The Digital Per-

Figure Out Which Record Label

formance Right in Sound Recordings Act of 1995 passed by the US Congress entitles record labels, featured performers, and their band to receive royalties when their works are broadcast over the internet or other media.

This was a landmark event that created a new source of income for record labels and artists. In the US, records released before 1972 were not given a similar measure of copyright security as sound recordings; because of this, no royalties were payable to record labels or artists. Regarding the performance of masters, unlike when these recordings are played on the radio.

This implies that a music publisher/songwriter gets royalty for radio airplay in the US, while a record labels/artist does not. **S**ections of this law amended this for digital uses and directed the formation of Sound-Exchange as an approach to gathering and paying out royalties in connection with them. While this new income stream is accessible, sadly, no royalty is yet payable to owners of masters or backup/featured artists when their sound recording copyrights are performed on terrestrial radio.

The splits between artists and recording labels depend on the following factors:

- The success and pull of the artists, regardless of whether the artist is new to the industry or an established superstar.

- Whether the artist is signed to a major record label or an independent record label.

If the record label is a major label, the artist's split can go from 13% to more than 20%. These arrangements will regularly accompany album advancements. For independent record labels, the split is usually 50% yet will frequently exclude an artist advancement.

CONCLUSION

The landscape of the music industry and music business has experienced remarkable changes over the last couple of decades. Not many will remember the age of vinyl records, cassettes or 8 tracks. Today, we are at a crucial turning point in the evolution of music where we stream our music from various streaming apps – all thanks to technology. We can rest assured that with steady advancements in technology, the industry will continue improving. It is therefore imperative that artists who will thrive should be open-minded and positioned to harness available platforms and tools to enhance their visibility to a wider audience while producing good music.

Although the music industry looks glamorous from the outside, with many high-profile names receiving the promise of fame and fortune from major record labels but ending up with just the fame and not the fortune for different reasons. As much as you want the fame and glitz that comes with being a player in this business, you also need to educate yourself and understand how contracts work.

Initially, it was difficult to imagine Independent music flourishing in the midst of major record labels and their artists. Nowadays, indie artists can hold their own against their counterparts financially and in other areas. With a clear vision and the right team, many indie artists have succeeded and made a name for yourself in the music industry.

There are various record deals in the marketplace. As an artist, you do not get what you deserve; no one will hand this to you except you negotiate favorable terms for yourself. Negotiating a great deal largely depends on your leverage – how well you prove that you are an asset. This is one reason why artists must build up their career before approaching a record label for a record deal.

REFERENCES

http://www.musicthinktank.com/mtt-open/a-brief-history-of-the-music-industry.html

https://syncopatedtimes.com/a-history-of-the-music-business-and-where-its-headed-now/

https://medium.com/@algoatwork/evolution-of-the-music-industry-the-three-3-elements-of-growth-189fe3da2b6

https://medium.com/the-brothers/this-is-how-they-rob-you-or-michael-jackson-was-right-603ced1503e0

https://variety.com/1997/biz/news/braxton-sues-laface-arista-over-contract-1116679450/

https://www.theguardian.com/music/2015/aug/10/history-prince-contractual-controversy-warner-paisley-park

https://www.theguardian.com/music/2017/jun/24/tlc-will-never-forget-day-we-were-millionaires-for-five-minutes

https://www.billboard.com/articles/news/73317/backstreet-boys-sue-zomba-for-75-million

https://www.masterclass.com/articles/how-do-synthesizers-work

https://www.billboard.com/articles/news/78564/dixie-chicks-sue-sony/

https://www.cbsnews.com/pictures/musicians-v-record-labels-famous-feuds/5/

https://www.musicindustryhowto.com/what-is-indie-music/

https://official.fm/indie/#:~:text=In%20general%2C%20indie%20music%20features,and%20drums%20with%20harmonized%20vocals.

https://theconversation.com/explainer-indie-music-28321

https://medium.com/the-brothers/this-is-how-they-rob-you-or-michael-jackson-was-right-603ced1503e0

https://indepreneur.io/blog/5-independent-musicians-refuse-sign-major-record-label/

https://www.openmicuk.co.uk/advice/recording-contracts-explained/

http://performermag.com/band-management/contracts-law/independent-label-vs-major-label-contracts/

https://www.soundonsound.com/music-business/recording-contracts-explained

https://www.newstatesman.com/culture/music-theatre/2020/07/i-lost-my-identity-artists-who-left-major-record-deals-form-their-own

http://bartdaylaw.com/net_profit_deals/

https://www.omarimc.com/10-types-of-record-deals-every-musician-needs-to-know/

https://soundcharts.com/blog/splits-and-profits-record-deals-analysis

https://medium.com/@jackconte/pomplamoose-2014-tour-profits-67435851ba37

www.ingramcontent.com/pod-product-compliance
Lightning Source LLC
Chambersburg PA
CBHW070948180426
43194CB00041B/1712